Bridges in Spirituality

First Nations Christian Women Tell Their Stories

Sarah Simon
Dr. Jessie Saulteaux
Gladys McCue Taylor
Gladys Taylor Cook
Vi Smith

as told to Joyce Carlson
and Alf Dumont

Anglican Book Centre
Toronto, Canada

THE UNITED CHURCH
PUBLISHING HOUSE
Toronto, Canada

Bridges in Spirituality
First Nations Christian Women Tell Their Stories

Canadian Cataloguing in Publication Data

Main Entry under title:

Bridges in spirituality : first nations Christian women tell their stories

Includes bibliographical references.

ISBN 1-55134-063-1

1. Indian women - Canada - Religion. 2. Feminist spirituality - Canada. 3. Indian women - Canada - Biography. 4. Christian women - Canada - Biography. I. Simon, Sarah, 1901– . II. Carlson, Joyce. III. Dumont, Alf.

E78.C2B74 1997 248'.089'97071 C97-930499-7

Anglican Book Centre
600 Jarvis Street
Toronto, Ontario
Canada M4Y 2J6
416-924-9192

United Church Publishing House
3250 Bloor Street West, Fourth Floor
Etobicoke, Ontario
Canada M8X 2Y4
416-231-5931
bookpub@uccan.org

Designer: Gordon Szendry
Substantive Editor: Lu Cormier
Copy Editor: Ruth Chernia

Printed in Canada

1 2 3 4 5 03 02 01 00 99 98

Cover image: This morning star quilt was created by Gladys Taylor Cook and Dorothy Elk to honour Laverne Jacobs, former Indigenous Ministries Coordinator, Anglican Church of Canada. Morning star quilts are part of the Dakota tradition and are given at births, deaths, and special celebrations. The colours of the quilt reflect Jacobs' strengths—the rays going from lighter to darker show honour and respect.

Photographs of Sarah Simon, Dr. Jessie Saulteaux, Gladys McCue Taylor, and Vi Smith courtesy of the elders and their families. Photograph of Gladys Taylor Cook © Keywest Photo.

970240

Contents

Women

A tree symbolizes
strength, beauty, courage,
by weathering storms, as in life
The branches,
her children, family, and friends,
nourished by love and care.
Spiritually spread through the roots,
secured by fulfilment of peace.

Gladys Taylor Cook

Foreword

We are moving to the end of the Ecumenical Decade of Churches in Solidarity with Women declared by the World Council of Churches (1988–98). In the search for a balance between women and men in the global context, there remains much work for our churches to accomplish. Especially challenging in this dialogue is how to involve women who are indigenous elders. This collection about women elders is an important resource for the ongoing work of the Decade.

The UN, in solidarity with the marginalized and oppressed, has declared the period from 1994 to 2004 the Indigenous Peoples Decade. The establishment of this decade came out of a Summit of Indigenous Peoples that met in October of 1993. A second resolution from the Summit reads:

> To recognize that our sister Rigoberta Menchu Tum, in her capacity as the Nobel Peace Prize Laureate, and due to her tireless struggle in favour of the rights of indigenous peoples, and to her vast experience with the United Nations in this sphere, carries the moral and technical authority necessary to coordinate this United Nations decade of the Rights of Indigenous Peoples, and to propose that she be appointed as the United Nations Goodwill Ambassador for this Decade.

With an indigenous woman identified for her work in the United Nations Decade, there is a new level of recognition of the gifts of women. Women who bless our communities with their gentle strength and healing are being acknowledged. The women in this book are creative leaders who bring hope to our lives.

These women elders remind us of the grandmothers, the aunts, and the many women who have marked our lives by their wisdom. These are the ones who carry us until birth and nurture us on the journey of life.

We have reached a moment when we remember that the gift of life on earth for humans is maintained by the strength of mothers. Those who encounter the stories of indigenous women elders in this book will be blessed.

Stan McKay

ACKNOWLEDGEMENTS

We wish to express our appreciation to the following individuals and groups for generously providing funding assistance in the publication of this book.

Diocese of Rupert's Land
Anglican Foundation
The Fellowship of the Maple Leaf
Anglican Council of Indigenous Peoples
Manitoba Community Services Council
The United Church Publishing House
Division of Mission, The United Church of Canada
All Native Circle Conference
Urban Rural Missions, World Council of Churches
Bay of Quinte Conference United Church Women
Regent's Park United Church Foundation
St. Stephen's Broadway Foundation of Winnipeg
Westennial United Church Foundation
Leyah McFadyen
Nancy's Very Own Foundation
Betty Ann Caldwell

To the elders and their families, we owe a special debt of gratitude. We have enjoyed their hospitality and friendship, and we have been richly blessed by being welcomed into their lives and stories. The elders' strong desire in sharing their stories was to contribute to greater understanding of First Nations cultures in Canadian society.

In accordance with the wishes of the storytellers and their families, authors, and editors, royalties from the sale of *Bridges in Spirituality* will be directed to ongoing development and sharing of First Nations stories.

The Diocese of Rupert's Land had a special part in the development of this book. Special thanks to Carol Throp, Karen Stuart, Cathy Mondor, and Bishop Pat.

Judy Delorme and the All Native Circle Conference, Council on Healing encouraged sharing of residential school experiences.

The Residential Schools Working Unit of the Anglican Church of Canada provided funding for a small group of women, including Gladys Cook, Phyllis Keeper, and Mina Stevenson to meet. This group provided insights that have guided this and many other publications.

This project has been in process for some time, in part because of changes in First Nations communities as well as in our churches. Stan McKay and Laverne Jacobs of First Nations Ecumenical Liturgical Resources, History and Publications Board shared a vision to affirm the giftedness offered by the elders. Donna Bomberry of Anglican Council of Indigenous Peoples has been encouraging. We are grateful to Bishop Jack Sperry for offering background and insights into the manuscript of Sarah Simon. Frank Saulteaux, Bernice Saulteaux, and Rhonda Taylor assisted with the manuscripts of their mothers.

Alf Dumont and Joyce Clouston Carlson

INTRODUCTION

Once in a while in our lives there are moments when the transcendent breaks through our ordinary daily lives. At such a time, the Mystery draws near. I remember clearly the first time this happened in my life.

I was crouching on a little path that led between the house and the barn on the small farm my parents' had carved out of the wilderness in the Interlake area of Manitoba. I was very young, perhaps two or three years, and my parents were tending the animals, or busy with other farm work. I waited for them on the path and busied myself with making tiny make-believe animals and little pens to keep them in, just as my parents were doing in the big barnyard beside.

I was surrounded on all sides by trees and woodlands. Our farm was in an area particularly rich with wild fruits, with saskatoons, chokecherries, pincherries, raspberries, and wild plums. I could hear birds flitting in the trees, and I could hear my parents' steps from a great distance. I heard the gentle tug as the cows reached for the long grasses that tempted them beyond the barbed wire on my side of the fence, the strain of their weight against wire. At a particular moment I suddenly looked up and saw the sun streaming through trees above making dappled shade on the path all around, moving in a wonderful harmony, through birdsongs, and the tug tugging of cows on long grasses, the whisper of the aspens in wind and I knew myself to be at one with the universe. I was separate and yet a part of everything.

It was as real, as touchable as the little pens I was making for my make-believe animals, and it struck me so deeply I felt dizzy. I dashed towards the house. At the end of the path I stopped, blinked in dazzling sunlight and wondered what had happened.

I now believe this to have been a transcendent moment, a moment when the Great Mystery, the Divine Otherness is near. Such moments have occurred again and again in the writing and editing of these stories. It happened as I walked with Sarah

Simon in Fort McPherson, watching as her friends and neighbours in the community that loved her stopped to chat while in the distance her beloved mountains rose, and a huge raven cried and lit upon a fence post beside us.

Such a moment occurred on a hillside in the Qu'Appelle Valley when Dr. Jessie Saulteaux described the northern lights coming down to meet the dancers on the night her mother died. At Jessie's funeral I felt the deep rhythm of the drum, her dancing spirit. I stayed once with Gladys McCue Taylor, watching the sun setting over a sacred island across the waters as she gently rocked her grandchild.

When I looked with Vi Smith out her living room window at Stekhoodinahl Mountain as she told me the Legend of the Mountain Goats of Damlaxan, a legend carried within her family from the time of the flood ten thousand years ago, I marvelled at the memory of her people who call themselves the "people of the mist," and who know so completely their place in the world. She pointed out the plain of Damlaxan in the mountains where the legend took place, and where she'd camped as a child.

I felt I knew Gladys Taylor Cook because we have worked so closely together over the past few years in a variety of projects. But, there came a moment when I suddenly gained a deeper appreciation of the life experience she had that brought the profound awareness of what "living in this world" is all about. When she described unconditional love, my only response was silence and, in that silence, I had yet another glimpse of the transcendent.

With each of the elders, one has a sense of wisdom and experience out of which eldership is born. To walk with each woman has been enriching, a growth of the soul.

My own mother died suddenly during the writing of this book. She passionately believed that the First Nations women who formed relationships with early explorers and traders were an important part of her own identity. She intuitively understood that something was missing from our own family and community when the First Nations women were unnamed and their contributions unaffirmed.

An artist, she painted their faces emerging from darkened canvas. This writing explores the rich spirituality and cultures of those women, bringing them to light. My hope is that it will assist all Canadians to affirm the important contributions of First Nations women to the stories of all our families and to the development of this country.

The opportunity to share in the writing and design with Alf Dumont has been deeply satisfying. Alf is in touch with the work of the soul. The balance of male and female, and the wisdom of his years in ministry, as well as experience in the All Native Circle Conference and the Dr. Jessie Saulteaux Resource Centre in their formative years, brought a real creative spark to our work together.

Joyce Carlson

Elders

We sat in the circle, struggling with future directions; we looked to the elders. After a long silence, Gladys Taylor finally spoke in words which have continued with me:

> As elders, we are not here to tell you what to do. As young people, as leaders, you are to determine your own directions. All we as elders can do is to tell you our stories, what we have done. You are asked to listen and to take from our stories what you need. Then, as leaders, you must determine where you are to go, and what you are to do. That is your responsibility.

Then Johnston Garrioch, with the sparkling laughing eyes of eldership, which were seared into my memory like glowing coals on a birch bark scroll, spoke: "And we will be watching you."

I have always been affirmed by the elders, even when I have made mistakes. They have never belittled me. When I stumbled on the way I was going or in the way I was leading others, they took me aside and were gentle with me. They told me stories and encouraged me to continue on my journey. They taught me to listen, by listening to me, by sharing with me in silence and by sharing my journey. They have defined eldership as a gentle caring for my spirit, my mind, and my body. They have taught me to braid my life together that way, as they braided their hair and as they braided the hair of Mother Earth [sweetgrass].

Throughout my life I have not known how elders came to be elders. I do know, that as I travel in the way of the spirit, elders have always been there. The Spirit of Life provides for us elders. They appear when we are in need of their gentle teachings. Not all older people are elders for us. Certain people who have journeyed in a certain way chose to become our elders, at the same time that we chose to be guided by them. At least, that is the way that it has happened in my life.

The elders I have known do not have an easy road to walk. They have always walked in the spirit of humility and with the spirit of integrity all their lives. They have sought to live by the gentle teachings of those who have been elders for them. Through their humour, reflection on their own lives and what has happened to them, and from the teachings that they have gained from those who went before them and guided them, they seek to guide those of us who will listen to them.

Often the stories they tell for the situations we are facing may not make sense to us at the time. We are asked to reflect on the story that we are told, until we can see what is being taught. We are not to raise questions until we have lived with the story for some time and listened to it many times to gain the wisdom that has been offered. To hear the truth and understand the truth and then to apply the truth may take months or even years. But the elders are patient and are watching.

I have been taught by many elders, but not too many. I have been told that one should not have too many elders. It would be too confusing to a developing soul. I am grateful for the teachings that I have received and am still receiving from the stories that have been shared with me by elders such as Gladys Taylor, Murray Whetung, Edith Memnook, Johnston Garrioch, Moses Wood, and Sandy Beardy.

There is so much to say about elders and eldership.

Alf Dumont

Sarah Simon

Recorded and edited by Joyce Carlson

Sarah Simon, a small, wiry woman with sparkling eyes, was born May 1, 1901. She bursts with energy, even in her nineties, and her bright eyes mirror the astonishing light of the midnight sun in her beloved north. Her people, the Gwich'in, the northernmost of the Dene Nation, are an Athapaskan speaking people, living along the Mackenzie, which they refer to as The Great River, and three very large lakes, the Athabasca, Great Slave, and Great Bear. Gwich'in peoples originally lived in the Mackenzie delta area, in lands that include the Northwest Territories, the Yukon, and what is now Alaska. In their own language, Dene means 'the people.' Their culture has developed and adapted in this area over thousands of years, with differing parts of the Nation adapting to the specific environment in which they lived, and developing a distinct language.

The lives of the people depended on having access to large expanses of land. An intimate knowledge of the land, of plant life, and of animals that they harvested for their survival was absolutely essential. Their highest regard was for those with the greatest knowledge.

The far north was the place of most recent encounters between traders and missionaries and First Nations peoples.

Sarah lost her mother when she was just two :

When I had my first baby, I saw my baby and cried and cried. I was brought up all alone and with no other children. At the same time, only on the day my baby was born, I felt that I had no mother. My mother died, I was told, when she gave birth to the baby after me.

It was only that day that I felt I had no mother. I thanked God that I had a daughter of my own. I didn't know she wasn't my own to keep; when she was 14 years old, she passed away. After my daughter died, four years later, I had a baby girl. That is the one who is living now. Five years later I had a baby boy. He died when he was five years old. A measles epidemic came around and he died.

So there is happiness and sadness. I am all alone and yet not alone. I am happy—trying to be happy.

Sarah was raised by her grandmother, her mother's mother. Gwich'in people were a hunting and gathering society who lived in small hunting groups, often consisting of related families living in comparative isolation, with specific times for social gatherings in their traditional life. Martha McCarthy described the life of the Dene during this period in *From the Great River to the End of the Earth.* In more recent times, their isolation was broken by gatherings at festivals such as Christmas and Easter, as well as the end of the trapping season. The land was not suitable for agriculture, although the people gathered berries. Food was plentiful most years, but large groups could not live in any one area without exhausting the resources. Sarah's young life was spent travelling with a small hunting group.

The first traders and missionaries who arrived met a community that was autonomous and whole. Although we have heard many stories of the first contact between early fur traders and missionaries, we have rarely heard those stories from the point of view of First Nations. They greeted the newcomers with welcome, some pity, and curiosity.

The society was an oral society, with teaching by story and example. Sarah's grandmother, a respected elder with considerable influence, remembered the arrival of the first traders:

I always think that when the first Hudson's Bay people came down here, the poor men must have been lonesome. There was no one to talk to, and their food was different. So finally, some of them married Native women. The girls didn't like white older men. They ran away from them.

My grandmother said that the first time she saw the white people, she was scared of them. The first white child was born years and years ago. She said that they didn't know anything about a white child. There was one girl that a Hudson's Bay man wanted to marry. There was no minister here in those days. So, he had this girl staying with him. But, the girl was scared of him. She always ran away on him. At last she really ran away and her parents sneaked away into the bush away up the creek so he never had a chance to get her again.

They gave her to another Native young man so she wouldn't have to go back to him. But, she was already pregnant.

My grandmother said that one day her mother was out in the night. She came home and said there was a baby born to this woman, but it was a funny kind of a baby and no one understood what it looked like. Everyone went to see that baby, the first white child.

The baby looked like a baby, all right, but the skin was all wrinkled just like something that was boiled. My grandmother was a little girl then and she begged her mother to go and see the baby. She was a relative of the girl and so she said, "Could I see my brother?" And so her mother took her to see the baby. But she was frightened. She said it was white and looked funny.

Later on, the young woman came back here and the older man was really sorry that the girl wouldn't stay with him. He left, but, he always sent something back. He sent clothing and things later on. When the baby was baptized, he talked to the minister here and wanted to give him his name, William Smith.

Indians didn't know about the true God yet, and they weren't married and the woman was scared of him. The people felt safe with their own kind. That is why the daughter went to an Indian man, and he was a good man to her.

The minister baptized him with the name William Smith. I knew him really well. He died quite a few years ago. He was the first white child and my grandmother was afraid. Later, she married my grandfather and her own children were white. I don't know how she managed with such funny children.

Sarah's grandmother also married a "Bay man." Sarah describes the circumstances of the marriage:

My grandmother lived to be 95 years old. She died in 1926. My grandfather died October 1891 on this lake. He drowned on this lake and is buried in the cemetery. My grandmother said that my grandfather, a Hudson's Bay man, talked the Native language before he married her.

They got married by the church. She said he wanted to marry her older sister, but the older sister didn't want to marry the man. She was scared. So, her mother told him to marry the younger. They just did it in this way.

When Sarah was nine, her grandmother became blind. An elder of the community, she knew the story of the community, and carried the wisdom. Young Sarah from her earliest memories took her grandmother's hand and led her where she needed to go, listening all the while:

Every evening I led her to church, to evening prayers until I was confirmed. Then I took her to communion. My grandmother remembers the first missionary. She remembers how he started his ministry. I remember quite well. She told her grandchildren and her sons. Many times I heard her telling about how the first missionaries arrived.

I couldn't say what year the first missionary came. The first missionary that came here was a Roman Catholic priest. He came and worked here hard then went over the mountain. But my grandmother said she was with another tribe of people and she didn't see him.

The rivalry between the Oblate Missionary Society and the Anglican Church Missionary Society is documented by Martha McCarthy, in chapter 4 of *From the Great River*, "Rivals in Faith." Hudson's Bay Company policy was to maintain impartiality, but a natural alliance formed between the mostly Scots, Orkney traders and Anglican missionaries in these far reaches of the British Empire. The Catholic Oblate missionaries of Belgian and French background, with their allegiance to the Pope, were viewed with considerable suspicion. The Protestant Hudson's Bay traders with allegiance to the Queen, often undermined the influence of the Catholic missions, favouring the Anglican.

The next summer the Hudson's Bay man told the people that there was a real minister coming, a real man who was going to tell them all the good news. This trader had a Native woman living with him. He told this woman about God the Father up in heaven. This woman told my grandmother about this. She finally believed that there was a God up in heaven who looks down on everywhere.

This description of the Anglican missionary as a "real man" may be a reference to the way in which Hudson's Bay employees undermined the Roman Catholic missions, suggesting the Catholic wasn't "real," or it may refer to the prevailing view within this Gwich'in hunting culture, which was that a man wasn't a real man unless he had a wife and children. It was difficult for the people to understand the idea of celibacy. This was a concept quite foreign to their way of living. The impartiality of the traders to the missions was circumvented by the energetic influence of a local woman, the wife of the Hudson's Bay trader, Flett. McCarthy gives more information on the influence of the Flett family on the success of the Anglican Mission at Fort McPherson.

This Hudson's Bay man, whose name was Mr. Flett, taught her about God. He told her the missionaries were in Alaska and he … asked if she was willing to tell the people about God, someone up above looking after people. This woman was beginning to learn everything about English from her husband. So they came back from Fort Yukon to here. When they came back here, already there were lots of people.

There were lots of people. There were so many people that this hill was covered with skin tepees, and down the bank too. This Hudson's Bay man told his wife, this woman, to tell all the people that there was a man coming, a true man coming to teach them about it.

He had three young people working for him. This woman had two or three children. These young people looked after the children and Mr. Flett let his wife from morning to evening talk to the people. They always had in one community a chief or head man to keep them in order. They depended on the chief for everything.

She talked to the head man about the true God as her husband told her. They were beginning to be very serious about the man who was coming to talk about the true God. He sent a message out. He sent boys all over to tell everyone to come here for that wonderful man coming. They had a big York boat coming. It was past spring in Fort Good Hope.

My grandmother was just a little girl and she listened to all this and was beginning to be interested in what she would hear. She always tried to be near this woman. She ran there before everybody could come. Finally, the boys saw the boat coming. The boys usually went down as far as you could see, 12 miles. Five or six boys went down. One man paddled in a little canoe to bring the news of who was on the boat. This man came and said that the speaker was coming. We call our preacher "speaker"—someone who will talk to the people.

Anyone who addressed a gathering of people was a speaker. Prior to the arrival of missionaries, the word was for any respected leader. In early days of missionary work, the word was used interchangeably to describe lay and ordained workers.

The people were very anxious to hear what they have to be told. The boys brought the boat up with tracking line, there was no other way from upstream. Finally they landed down there. There were so many people! My grandmother said she couldn't come close enough to see this man coming up the bank. She just couldn't see this man coming up the bank. There were two Hudson's Bay men with him. This woman said, "Move everything, make way for this man to come up."

My grandmother said that she started crawling among people's legs. So much she crawled. Finally she came to a trunk so she couldn't stand up. So, she sat there watching this man come up.

She saw the man coming, a little short man with a nice little blue coat and a little straw hat. He had a cane and was carrying something. It was really queer. They couldn't make out what it was that he was carrying. Maybe it was just a little briefcase. I don't know. Nobody, no one knew about paper, books or anything like that.

In those days, the Eskimo and Loucheaux people had wars. Sometimes they attacked one another. So they had to watch from a little hill where there were no trees so they could see 12 miles up if the Eskimos were coming by boat. Then, if they saw someone coming, they could get ready.

The first missionaries arrived in the 1860s. Sarah refers to her own tribe as Loucheaux, a derivative of a French word that translates roughly as 'squint-eyed.' The eyes of the people are described as lovely to those who know the people. The name is less used now by younger generations. Loucheaux, however, continues to be used by elders like Sarah, and so this text respects her own usage.

The Gwich'in lived at the top of the Mackenzie delta, next to those she refers to as 'Eskimo,' which means 'those who eat uncooked meat.' Their eating of raw meat has enabled them to survive for centuries; vitamin C is retained in raw meat, and they therefore didn't develop the scurvy that killed many early European arrivals. The people Sarah calls Eskimo refer to themselves as *Inuvialuit,* meaning 'the people' in their own language. Historically, the Inuvialuit and Gwich'in had been enemies. Sarah describes the choice of location of the first missionary's talk at a height of land that allowed the people to see afar, to know if danger was approaching:

Where the Hudson's Bay store is and Hudson's Bay house, they built a fort, a big fence with long pillars. In the corners they built a fort like a house where they made a place where they could have guns. If the Eskimo attacked, the men would run into that place and shoot them. Eskimos didn't know anything about guns and if they heard a shot, they ran away.

More recent missionaries have said that the enmity between these Nations was well known, although they do not recall an actual outbreak of hostility. The presence of the traders and missionaries may have encouraged reconciliation between the Nations. However, the historic enmity certainly lived in the memory of the people, and the meeting place was known by local peoples in this way:

So there was the hill there. This woman told the people make way, make way for the speaker to walk through. And the Hudson's Bay man met him and was taking him home. The woman told the people, "Wait, this man is very tired. He has to have something to eat with my husband. After that he will come out and talk."

But the people wouldn't go home. They wouldn't leave. They just stayed there. They went into Hudson's Bay House and after they had something to eat, she came out again my grandmother said. There were three stools there to sit on, one for [the] Hudson's Bay man, one for the minister and one for [the] woman. This was way up on top of the Fort.

They sat down there and she came out and told them, "You people try to sit down, sit down on the ground and listen. This man will talk..." and they did. He brought out some kind of paper and she hung it up on that wall and he took his cane and pointed. And no one had seen anything like that before.

This was in the morning, early in the morning. For lunch, they went in again and the people wouldn't leave. Then after lunch, they came out and it was the same thing again. They learned about the word of God.

They didn't know what the words meant. For days they went on from morning to evening. As soon as the minister went into the house, all the people turned around and said, what did he say, what did he say? She said she was a little girl. She remembered words. People around her would surround and ask her, "What did he say?" and she would repeat the words.

After seven days this woman told the people, "This man and the Hudson's Bay men are going over the mountain." They walked on foot, they walked on ground. They were going by boat across the river and packing their food and their belongings in a dog pack. She said that he would go and teach like this every place that he stopped in the Yukon. Then, in the fall time before it gets too cold, the Hudson's Bay people would come back and he would come back and he would stay for a while to teach again.

Until then, he had to leave now. He had to leave the next day. Everyone was to go home. But, they never moved. They stayed right there. Then they took him across the river. The head man got up and shouted, "What will you people do for the winter? You have stayed here all this time, even without eating. You better try and put fish up, make dried fish for the winter. Everybody has to leave."

In September, they said, the speaker was coming back, and the Hudson's Bay men were coming back. They sent a man ahead days before they were coming, and the message came back, "They are coming!"

As soon as they got the word, everybody came back here. Now, they had dried fish. When they saw the smoke up on the hill, that meant they were coming back and everybody was ready. This woman all summer long worked with people. She went out to the camps and told everyone about the person who came, saying that whatever he said was true. This is what her husband told her and she believed.

We asked my grandmother, "What do you mean by the first word, in the beginning?" She said, "It was many, many years ago and I can't remember. You have your Bible, why don't you look it up? Look for it," she told me. I said, "In St. John, chapter one...In the beginning, the word was with God."

"Oh! That's the one! that's the one!" she said! "Many old people memorized that chapter. If I asked an old person what they wanted me to read, they always said the first word."

Gwich'in peoples, particularly the elders, had well-trained minds, a capacity necessary to maintaining their oral tradition for centuries. They told stories that revealed the truth of their own lives and also gave others the opportunity to learn as much as they were able to grasp from the stories. The ability to recall continues to this day, with many able to recite long biblical passages and sing through entire hymn books.

He came back here and in the same way again for seven days and talked day after day. This woman translated for him whatever her husband taught her. This man said that he had to go back up the Mackenzie River to Fort Simpson, the headquarters of the church and the Hudson's Bay people.

That was where he was going back to and he told the people that he was going back home, but next spring or early summer, there was a man coming in to teach them, to stay with them.

So this man who was called Kirby taught them again and then he left. All through the winter people who remembered words had other people around come to them. The next summer, the boat came and Reverend McDonald, a young boy, came. My grandmother said he was just a very young boy. So, he came and he started the work, he started teaching.

Robert McDonald would have been in his twenties at the time of his arrival at the mission. An important missionary in the north, McDonald was of mixed race origins from Red River.

This woman never stopped. She always was telling the people what her husband said about these things. Later on, my grandmother got married to my grandfather. In 1859, my grandmother got married by the missionaries. They didn't live together like before because now they had religion.

Sarah's family embraced Christianity and tended to negate the belief system that had guided their lives previously. Prior to the arrival of missionaries, the people had their own deep religious beliefs. Religion was an integral part of their society, and was reflected in their relationships to each other, their economy, and society. The spirit world was very real and very near, and a way of dealing with the world was through the observance of taboos, particularly around hunting. Dreams were very important. If, for example, starvation occurred, blame might be attached to a certain person, and the results could be both difficult and vicious, yet understandable within their cultural frame of reference.

Arranging suitable marriage partners in this hunting society was critical, since the very survival of a young couple depended upon the skill and reliability of a prospective partner. Elders taught about acceptable social behaviour, especially marriage and sharing. On the arrival of missionaries and with the acceptance of Christianity, the union was formalized in a church. Until very recently, marriages were still often arranged by parents and elders. Later, if missionaries were trusted and respected in their communities, they were often consulted and asked to assist in making decisions about such matters as arranging marriages.

Even in my young days, the Indians arranged the marriages. They didn't leave it up to the young people to choose one another. In fact, we didn't talk to one another before we were married. But, I was a bad girl. I was different. I talked to my boy.

Even in Sarah's childhood, rules about prescribed behaviour were beginning to change. Sarah's grandmother, having married a trader with the Hudson's Bay Company, began to integrate European ideas into her own life and family. She also internalized some of the very British values of the Anglican Church:

I was brought up by my grandmother who was very fussy about everything. She taught me never to sit in church with nothing on my head. Always wear something on my head. They carried on like that. The women weren't to speak up among the people. The women had to be the last all the time. Yet, so many women learned to read and write and helped their people.

Sarah heard the words of Christ in terms of the role of women in her society, a society living on the land in one of the harshest environments in the world. Her comment about the women being last may reflect the role of women in a culture that had been entirely reliant on the success of the hunt. Women worked very, very hard. Because this was a hunting economy, the hunter was a very important person, and this could lead to abuses. The life of the wife or wives depended in large part on whether the hunter was kind. While some were kind, others could be quite cruel. Particularly if the community were under stress, a woman's life might be at risk.

Christianity became well established, and quickly. Sarah, through her grandmother's sharing, felt that the women in particular understood the liberating words of Christ, welcoming missionaries:

The first words of the Bible was a few words of John the Gospel, maybe just a verse. Then they learned a few more words.

My grandmother really memorized the prayers. She said her prayers as if she were reading the church prayers. Archdeacon McDonald lived with the people and that is how religion spread. He chose the young boys and tried to teach them. In olden days, the women were nothing. Indians were like that. The women were not to go ahead of the men. But now the women were the head. They were the ones who memorized the things they were taught.

Sometimes, many families went together for the winter and from early November until June and we didn't see them in town at all. They were out. The lay people taught their own people. They did a lot of good work. Archdeacon McDonald taught the Loucheaux here and taught in different parts of the Yukon and all over Alaska. That is why we use Loucheaux books all over.

Many things were memorized without books. But, the very first words that were used were that "The word was with God and the word was God."

In spite of the difficulty of women's lives, and their place as last, as Sarah describes, a wise woman, particularly an elder woman like Sarah's grandmother, might have traditionally had a great deal of influence in the community. With the coming of Christianity, women in the camps caring for children quickly embraced the new teachings. They learned to read, using the translation work being done by McDonald, and carefully considered these new teachings.

McDonald translated the entire Bible into Gwich'in, a formidable task. The Gwich'in language is complex and tonal, similar to Chinese, in which sound is very important. If the correct sound is not made, one could make serious mistakes. Very few non-Gwich'in peoples ever mastered the language. McDonald became a linguist and was greatly helped in his work by his wife.

Oblate missionaries felt that the marriage of McDonald to a local Gwich'in woman gave the Anglicans an unfair advantage. A story is told within Anglican circles of the circumstances of his marriage, which according to McCarthy had a significant impact. Prior to his arrival in the far north, he had been engaged, but the engagement had been broken by the young woman. He had been let down. While serving his mission, he was teaching a confirmation class, and found a young woman he favoured. When he expressed this to her, suggesting marriage, she was frightened and ran crying to her father, who took pity on her and refused permission for the marriage. McDonald had a second choice, a young woman who also ran crying to her father. However, her father told her that if she married him, she would always have enough food to eat; the father gave permission and they were married.

Anglican ledgers indicate that McDonald officiated at his own wedding. He and his wife Julia, who was related to many, many people, raised a large family and were much loved.

When Archdeacon McDonald started baptizing people, he baptized old people and young people among the Indians.

Archdeacon McDonald just travelled with the people and spoke not a word of English, while living with the Indians. One old woman said many times he stayed with her family in their tent. That is why she could read her books now. He taught her. At first, he had a hard time. As soon as he understood, it was good because he could teach in Loucheaux. He spent 40 years in the north.

Early missionaries lived among the people. In a way, they were like children of the people, learning from them the language, ways of behaving, and basic survival techniques. The people corrected them when they were wrong and encouraged them. Missionaries became central to the lives of the communities. Their ministry included becoming interpreters to the outside world, and acting as doctors and dentists, too. Their wives often became midwives.

Sarah was profoundly affected by the missionaries, including in the choice of her husband:

My husband was brought up in the Yukon. All the Loucheaux people moved over to the Yukon in Klondike days, 1892. He only came back to his country in 1916. His grandfather was a great Indian chief. His father was as well. They were a well-known family.

We had a minister named Archdeacon Whittaker. Mr. Whittaker spent 20 years here, down the coast and all over. He was my teacher. James, as a young boy, used to work for him. I grew up near the mission door. Many times the children didn't go out to school. There was no school in the village. My grandmother asked him if he could teach me more because he didn't want me to go out to school. He wanted me to stay with my grandmother. He promised that he would teach me. This is how I went to school.

They left in 1917 and even after they left, they always used to write to me. They called me their daughter and they wrote to me. He used to arrange marriages for young people. He always used to say, "Don't just marry someone who comes to McPherson, marry someone you know." He told me James Simon was a good boy who used to work for him. My father wanted me to marry him. I said I didn't want to. Archdeacon Whittaker wrote to me, he said to listen to my father. He told me to marry James and it would be good. But, I didn't want to.

For four years, he came and then he came again. Each time, he asked if I was going to marry him. I said no. Then in 1920, I made a big mistake! I used to tell my husband that. At last, I made up my mind. Then we got married here.

Although the suggestion was made about the choice of an appropriate marriage partner, Sarah participated in the decision making. It appears that others didn't feel the same freedom:

In those days, people listened to the church. They listened to the minister. What the minister said, had to be done. He arranged marriages for the young people. If Mr. Whittaker said, this is going to be a good husband, you had to marry him. He'd say, "He's a good boy, it's a good girl," and they had to do it.

I remember my grandmother told me that one old woman came to her and she told her "My daughter is really crying, doesn't want to marry that boy." The speaker said she should — "So what can I do?"

My grandmother said, "Go to my son-in-law and talk to him, find out what he says." This woman came back crying, and said, "He said it will turn out good—do it. What can we do?"

The next day, they got married. Not too long ago, that old woman died and all her sons and daughters have good homes. They are good people.

We used to have Indian names. I wrote [them] down for the lay readers. This time of the year we lived in tents. There were not many houses. Sunday afternoons, you could hear the women gathered together in their tents, singing hymns here and there to one another. Then, the bells rang for Sunday school, and children and even old people went to Sunday school.

Sunday we were not allowed to do any work. Sunday was the Lord's day. We had to go to church, then we just stayed home. We didn't do much. When Mr. Whittaker was our minister, he didn't allow anyone to work on Sundays.

Observance of rules for behaviour, such as not working on Sunday, appears to have been readily understood as for the common good, and incorporated into this society. They were used to observing taboos, particularly around the hunt. After Sarah married, she and her husband served as missionaries to the Gwich'in.

When we got married, I was only 19. I had gone to church day school, so I could read a little and write. When we got married, my husband could talk English, but he couldn't read English.

Oh, I felt bad about that! I felt, it's not fair. I thought everybody should be able to go to school. So I started teaching him, and he was very interested in what I told him. This is why we became missionaries.

We had a good marriage. We went back to school, up the Mackenzie [the Anglican Residential School at Hay River established in 1908]. That's where we went to school.

Her appreciation and longing for education is reflected in Sarah's desire for her husband to have an education as well. The first education in the north was often initiated by Hudson's Bay Company employees who pressed for education for their children. Sarah's family were Hudson's Bay people, and education was provided to Sarah by the Anglican missionary. It was the strong desire of the Bay employees, as well as the Métis who worked for the Oblates in their missions, to establish the early schools. The Church Missionary Society that supported many missionaries in the north also encouraged the establishment of schools. Missionaries as well as their wives were often the first teachers. Sarah describes her own schooling.

I was taught in English from six years old. My parents taught English all the time. When I got married, and we had a little girl, we talked to her in Loucheaux. When we went away to school, our other little girl was just two years old. We were told when we went to Hay River School that we were not to speak Loucheaux to our children. The principal said no other language but English. He wanted children to talk really good English. But the children didn't listen. They all kept their language.

When we went back to the boarding school, we were treated like little school children, my husband and I. But, whatever we were taught, I thank God that it was pretty well used. I was very happy and thankful that I went back to that school. My husband took the Bible. I took music lessons and church activities so I was taught about the church.

When Sarah and James were studying at Hay River, many people from other cultures—Inuvialuit as well as other Dene tribes—attended the school. English was their common language. During a Lenten season, the principal instructed everyone that only English language would be allowed at all times. This would imply that many were not following these rules.

Sarah was fluent in English, but the language of her husband's heart was Gwich'in. He had great difficulty with English. Knowing the struggle this would cause him, Sarah boldly went to the principal and asked, "And what language will you be speaking to your wife during Lent?" When he replied, "English," she said, "And I will speak to my own husband in his own language." The principal agreed they should be free to speak in their own language. One would think this particularly important in their prayer and study together, and Sarah was anxious that her husband have some of the opportunities for learning that she had had. Sarah ensured that her own children spoke Gwich'in although she also spoke to them in English.

Sarah was a very strong-minded person, and very well educated in a deep sense. Because of her linguistic abilities and her understanding of the people, she was able to hold her own with anyone, including government officials.

Just because I went back to school, my people thought that I knew so much. I didn't. I knew very little. But, the people thought I knew everything. In those days, there was no hospital near, no hospital in the north. The missionaries had a dispensary and they looked after the people. When the missionaries were gone, I did it. It is because I was doing things like that, my own auntie, Mrs. Firth, talked to me.

She told me she was getting on. She delivered lots of babies in town and in the bush. She couldn't do it very well any more. "You've been doing lots of good work," she said. "You take my place."

"Oh," I said, "I don't know how. I don't know what to do." She told me her own granddaughter was having her first baby coming. "My granddaughter is expecting any day now. When they call me, I'll come and pick you up." I was happy I was going to be with her. She showed me how to deliver a baby.

Then, the next week, her other daughter-in-law was delivering and she told me to do it myself. She sat there, but I delivered the baby. I delivered 86 babies myself in this town and up the Peel River. I've gone up and down by boat 30 miles and by dog-team 12 miles. I had to wake up at night. At night, when I was asleep, there would be a knock at the door and the husband would say, "My wife needs you."

My husband would say, "Hurry up, you are needed." And I told him, "After it is all over, I'll call you and you come and have prayers," and he would do this. This is how we worked. After everything was over, he would come and say prayers and give thanks.

Then a nurse came. She came on duty in September. When the first nurse came, I worked with her for a little while. I thought to myself, Oh I am so happy! At last, the nurse is going to be here. I was happy. I said to myself, now I'm going out with my husband. I'm going trapping and fishing with my husband. I'm not going to rush to McPherson or rush somewhere else.

The doctor came. The doctor checked up everything. I had to go with the doctor to talk with him. He said, "Now, Mrs. Simon, I want to talk to you. You've been working like this [as a midwife] for so long. Will you assist the nurse? She's only a young girl and doesn't know the people. She doesn't know the language. Could you assist her for a while?"

I said, "Don't you know I'm a married woman and I have to talk to my husband before I can say yes." So I came home and I talked to James. He looked at me. My husband said, "Well, it's your work, and if you want to do it, do it." Even though we had a hard time sometimes. We had to trap to make our living. He'd just take it like that.

We worked as trappers and hunters and missionaries. We got $200 worth of groceries for one year. Today if we got that, how far would it go? One hundred and fifty pounds of flour for one year. But, we got that much help and we trapped and we lived off the land. We did well. We brought up some homeless children and lots of times I put up old women and old men.

We travelled out in the bush and we came back to the town and we worked for the church as much as we could. We left the town after everybody left, we came back before everybody came back. This is what we used to do. We had a boat with a motor in it. When we went to Aklavik, we took people down sometimes. Sometimes patients, sometimes missionaries. We enjoyed doing things like that.

Because of rapid change in the north, and the many different dialects and languages, many people felt it was an advantage for children to learn English. When the children were sent away to school, the life of the people continued as it had for generations. Sarah describes the rhythm of this life:

When there was no school here, people sent the children elsewhere to go to school. Then, they travelled in the bush. On fifteenth of July, everybody goes away fishing. Up and down the river and down on the delta—and we dried fish, we made lots of dried fish for the winter and put them away. We dried them in the smoke house and after about the middle of August, it was hard to dry fish. We worked to put away berries for the winter.

Some of the people went [to] the mountains and whenever people were moving away from the town, like a big family, they would go to the missionary, they would ask to have a lay reader to stay with them and to have Sunday prayers, to have services with them. These lay people didn't get paid—but still, they listened to the church.

We were lay readers. Wherever the church sent us, we would go—on our own. So that is how we travelled around with the people. And, we would go to the fishing places, the camping places, and we would have Sunday services, morning and evening and a Wednesday evening or Friday evening. And, if I had time I taught the day school. I just did that because I loved to do it. We kept going, whatever we wanted to do with people, we talked to people and we would do it. It was easy to get along together that way. When we had plenty of fish, we would share that too.

And then, in September, we started putting away fish for winter and dog food. We had no vehicles here, just dogs, by dog-team. We burned wood, we stayed in tents, we lived off the land. That was a very good thing. The men would sit down and make snowshoes for winter time, fix up everything for the winter. The women were sewing winter clothing for the children, men, and for themselves. When the fall time came, we put nets under the ice. This is for eating fish. Now we put that frozen fish away. We had no freezers. We set rabbit snares. We killed lots of rabbits and put that away for winter. When the first of November came, then the trapping season opened. The time for women and men—and whoever was able to trap, we set out traps. We got fine fur.

As soon as we got a few furs, the husband came to Fort McPherson by dog-team and brought back groceries and whatever we needed. Then, we would be all right for another two or three weeks. We kept doing that. We killed lots of fur. In those days, there was lots of fur, too. But now we have to go far to get meat and fur. But we have other kinds of meat like rabbit and ducks. In the summertime, we put ducks away. We kept ourselves busy and happy. Once in a while we went to the next camp and visited one another. Sunday, sometimes people would come to our place and we had a service and gave them meat. In the evening after prayer, they would all go back home. We'd do that.

Then, the week before Christmas, everybody came, all the families. Then we had Christmas holidays in town. Men hauled wood in the morning, and you could hear the dogs howling everywhere, there was lots of noise. Across the lake, across the river, you could hear them bringing wood with dog-teams. Women set snares, women washed and sewed for Christmas. We made everything for Christmas. Not like the ready-made clothes today. We made all our dresses. We didn't say we were tired and didn't want to do it. We just had to.

When Christmas came, we had a special church service. The community put up a tree and we had a dance and dog races and sports like that. In the evening we visited one another and talked. There was no mischief. This is how we used to live.

Sarah and her husband had to cope with discouragement, too. Within their own community, they were sometimes criticized:

I tried very hard with whatever I had to do. James did this too. An old, old woman [told] me when we started working for the church, in my background there were never missionaries. And James, too, in his background there were no missionaries. Her husband was a lay worker and she thought her children should be doing missionary work. She asked, "Why are you doing that?" She told me this and it made me feel so bad. But, I didn't say anything to her.

So I told my mother-in-law what this old woman said. My mother-in-law said, how does she know that James' background was not missionary. We all learned our Bible. She said, "Read your Bible." Anybody who reads the holy word of God is a missionary.

My husband worked as a layman for 33 years. Oh! we worked hard. Now, I'm really glad I've done this. We used to go into the bush with other families. We would go up into the mountains, or anywhere to have a church service, to carry on Sunday prayers. I'm very fond of teaching Sunday school and doing the women's work. I tried to keep up with it even when we were travelling.

After serving many years together as lay ministers in the Diocese of the Arctic, James Simon was called to ordained ministry in the Yukon, and Sarah and James served several years there before retiring to their home in Fort McPherson in the Diocese of the Arctic.

My husband was an Anglican priest. He was ordained in the Yukon by Bishop Greenwood, and served there. We lived with the Bishop in the mission house. We taught him Loucheaux, and he taught us, too. He never forgot us.

In her lifetime, Sarah witnessed enormous change. During the winter of 1906 to 1907, there was a critical shortage of fur-bearing animals, together with severe weather, when sickness and famine affected all peoples of the Mackenzie. Every band relied on missionaries and the Hudson's Bay posts to survive. After several winters without adequate food, even minor illnesses could lead to death. Despite certain treaty agreements, there was limited assistance from the Canadian government. An oil discovery in the territories, interest in outsiders to exploit this resource, together with the desire by the Dene for increased medical supplies, education for their children, and assistance in caring for their old and destitute contributed to their desire for treaty.

Treaty was taken in 1921. Bishop Breynat of the Oblates had encouraged the taking of treaty in the hope that it would improve the life of the Dene, ensuring aid in time of need, and education for the future. In fact, it seemed, the government worked less closely with the people, and they felt less autonomy.

Sarah would have married around 1920, just before treaty was taken. Relationships between the Dene, the missionaries, and the

Hudson's Bay employees had been based on a mutual interdependence. Both Anglican and Catholic missions had relied quite heavily on lay ministers like Sarah and James, who adapted the teachings of Christianity to their own culture. Relationships with government were not as interdependent, and change was accelerated following the treaty process. Government policy was based on premises of western society and progress; the Dene rarely were consulted.

People had pressed for education in the belief that it would be advantageous to their children in preparing for change. But the Dene found having their children living separately from them was difficult. McCarthy's book details some of the impact of residential schools (see Appendix Two). Sarah describes her frustration with the change:

The school caused the life to change. Our school [the government-run school in Fort McPherson] was named after Chief Julius. I interpreted for Chief Julius many, many times. He cried for a school here. He wanted a school right here. Everybody wanted a school here. So the government finally brought a school here. Then, the people had to travel and the children had no place to stay. So, he started on the idea of having a hostel. The government built a big hostel here, and 200 children went there. A few years after we left here, we were away, hardly anyone went to the hostel. Children went to Inuvik or somewhere else and the hostel was far too big. The Indians tried to run it on their own for one year, but they couldn't do it without money. So we lost our hostel.

The hostel, which provided care for children attending school, was funded by the government but operated by the Anglican Church. The presence of the hostel allowed people to continue going out on the land and working on their trap lines while their children attended school. Those children wishing to go on to higher grades went to Inuvik, a distance of 120 km (80 miles). The Gwich'in did not find this easy, and so delayed the closing of the hostel by attempting to administer it themselves. This proved impossible.

Oh, it broke my heart to see it come down. So, they had no hostel. Since they had no hostel to place their children in, everybody stayed right in town. Then the town started to grow. There were not very many houses then, but then they were given houses, and pushed them away up here away from the church ground. Before that we all used to live right around the church.

Eventually the community of Fort McPherson grew and the higher level grades were available in the local schools. Children remained in their own homes to attend school. However, this meant that the people were not able to travel to their lands and live in their traditional way. Sarah sees this change in schooling as one that changed the lifestyle of the people.

From an independent people living off the land, they began living in settlements. This had some advantages, as the people had homes, but this meant that they were no longer independent, and working. There were immense political changes taking place as well:

The parents had to stay close for the children to go to school. I suppose they didn't *have* to give up the trapping, but sometimes there was no money in the fur. Then, they were also dealing with the land claims, land claims, land claims all the time. When I go on the place up in the air I look down on the delta, I always feel upset. There are so many good fishing camps, many good trapping areas, good lakes, good creeks, good rivers, all willows like this. Maybe it is not only me who feels this way. The ones that remember what a good life we used to have [also feel bad]. Now, to young people, living in town is very good for them, they like it. But, old people like us, while I hardly lived in the bush as much as other people, but I really enjoyed my life living off the land.

Lives of the people were changing, partly because of the changes brought by treaty, introduction of residential schools, laws requiring attendance at school, but also because of unanticipated changes. In her discussion of Oblate Missions, McCarthy suggests that Oblate missionaries were not aware of the profound ramifications that even minor change might have on people whose culture and religion were a unified whole.

It was also true that the people themselves welcomed some of the change, for example, assistance in times of great need. The change has profoundly affected the church as well. Until treaty was taken, the police, the Hudson's Bay Company, and the missions formed the centre of community life. With increasing involvement of the government, hospitals, hostels, and schools have come under the jurisdiction of the regional government. Gradually, the role of missions has changed to the spiritual, as well as some counselling.

Lives have really changed now. When I was growing up, even in the early forties, on Sunday mornings, no one stayed home. The church was packed. You could hear people singing away from the church. Wherever you were in town, you'd hear it. Now, when I look in the churches usually there aren't many [people].

When I was growing up, we were not allowed to play outdoors after dark in the winter. In the summer, we liked to stay outside, to play outdoors. But our parents said, no, this is night-time, you're not allowed to play outside after dark—after eight or nine or like that.

The old people used to tell the young people: "You know, there's a night watcher from above looking down on children, looking after the children. The angels are looking after you in the night-time. In daytime, they change. So, day and night somebody is looking after you from up in heaven. Don't do anything wrong, and don't stay out. Remember there is somebody watching you."

It would be extraordinarily painful for Sarah to witness the devastating changes around her in what had been a self-reliant settlement.

So, hardly any old people are living now who remember the old life. The young people like the modern life today, but they don't know how much they lost. I could look at it that way. Quite a few people are trapping still. My grandson now is trying hard to live off the land. He now has big boys and he trains them too. He takes them out in the bush and shows them what to do, some friends do that too. But, now there has been a fire where they used to trap and they don't know what will happen.

I really don't know what will happen now.

While children no longer learned how to hunt, fish, and trap from their parents, there were many new avenues open to them.

Their education gave them opportunities to meet potential partners, and so the parents and elders were no longer arranging their marriages or able to support them in this new way of approaching relationships. When the young had difficulties, parents no longer knew how to help. Marriages that had been upheld by the support of family and community broke down. Temporary relationships replaced formerly stable marriages and children were sometimes neglected.

Alcohol, first brought in as home-brew and later by licensed government outlets, destroyed the best of the old ways. As the whole society underwent enormous change, the lives of women, in particular, became increasingly difficult. It was not uncommon for women to be severely beaten. The young began to disobey their parents, or found little to respect in drinking parents. Their language had also almost completely disappeared. In McPherson, of a population of 800, it is estimated that only 40 might understand the language, and even fewer would be literate in it. Sarah struggled with the issue of language in her own family, with her own children.

So, I started talking English then to all my children. I talked only English to my youngest. The oldest lost her Loucheaux [Gwich'in] that she knew. By the time we came back here, I started working in the church, I found that I just couldn't make myself talk Gwich'in to them. When I talked my language, I'd say something, and then I'd have to repeat it in English. So, finally, I talked only English to my children and to James.

But living here among our own people, they couldn't help but understand Loucheaux right away. All my children did. My own daughter hardly lived down here. She went to school and we talked only English to her but she played and talked to all the children—and she speaks Loucheaux good. When she was in grade 10, we sent her out. We wanted her to have a good education. There was no high school at that time. We sent two of them out, her and one of my cousins, to go to Alberta College in Edmonton. So that's where my daughter went to high school. When she had another year to go and we moved to the Yukon, she came back home. She never hardly talked Loucheaux.

Two years later we were transferred to Old Crow. She lived with us for just a few months when the school superintendent wanted her to go to Inuvik School, a big school. So, she went there to supervise the boys and girls. There, she met her husband. He was going to high school. He just wouldn't wait. He wanted to marry her. So she wrote to me and told me about it. The school superintendent told me to talk to them, to tell them to wait. He wanted both of them to finish their high school. Susie was taking university and nurse's training—but this boyfriend wouldn't leave her alone. So they got married really young. They had a little boy, a little girl, a little boy, a little boy again. As soon as she weaned the little boy, she went back to school again—and I had to babysit.

My son-in-law went back to school too in Ottawa. Then he came back here. And yet, my daughter speaks really good Loucheaux even though I taught her in English. Parents should speak their own language at home. They are living in Yellowknife. She's an R.N. They are both working for the government and they have had a restaurant. They closed down their restaurant. She has a job as a nurse now.

Sarah's daughter eventually became employed as a Gwich'in translator. Sarah describes her and James' years in the Yukon:

He wanted to be a minister, but our Bishop in the Diocese of the Arctic didn't do anything. For 33 years he worked really hard. We both worked really hard for the church. Finally, God called him.

I used to tell him, "James, look here, you wait, you wait, wait for God! God will make the decision."

Once in a while, he said, "I am a trapper. I can hunt and we can feed our children more and better trapping than sticking around here and working for the people." Sometimes he got that way.

And I said, "Don't get carried away! Wait for God. Remember God is slow. When your time comes, it will come."

One day, the Bishop of the Yukon wrote. My husband was reading his mail. All at once, he just jumped up! "I'm going! I'm going! I'm going!" he said.

He gave me the letter. It was the Bishop of the Yukon calling him. This is how we got there.

In 1959, on October 18, he was ordained. When he was 60 years old, he was ordained an Anglican priest. After that, we spent seven years in Whitehorse. We lived with the Bishop in the Mission House. We taught him Loucheaux, and he taught us, too. He never forgot us. Bishop Greenwood had a service for the Church Army. My husband acted as Bishop's Chaplain. They met him and they were fond of him. We sold everything when we left home. My husband was so happy. He was brought up in the Yukon, but he never went back there since we were married. Now, he was called to the Yukon.

When James was ordained, the Anglican Church did not allow the ordination of women, but if they had, Sarah would most certainly have been ordained as well. She was an extraordinarily gifted woman.

When we retired, we came back to Fort McPherson to live here. It was a hard decision. When we were leaving, they asked what we needed for the church. They said they'd be glad to visit. Just before we left, we bought dishes for the women's auxiliary to use, and curtains to use at the back of the altar for different seasons, oh they looked so pretty, and the music for the belfry.

Old Crow is just a young village. It was a good fishing place, and good for caribou. After using it as a camp, later on, they lived there. In 1920, they built a church. They had minister after minister. In 1960, they built a new church. In 1961, we went there. We lived in Old Crow for four years. Another time we replaced a minister on vacation. The church is small, but always packed.

We tried hard to fix the rugs, to do sewing and make cushions from moose hair. We completed the church real good. I always feel happy when I go there.

The church at Old Crow is small, but very beautiful, as is the village itself. It is an isolated settlement near Fort McPherson that had been a temporary camp of Gwitch'in people during the caribou hunt. It was a particularly rich area, on a well-known migration route. So remote are these areas that Bishop Sperry recalls hearing that the people continued to pray for Queen Victoria, whom they had heard about from the early Church Missionary Society missionaries, even during the Russian occupation of Alaska and its subsequent sale to the United States. No one knew they were there.

Towards the end of her life, Sarah's perseverance in affirming the Gwich'in language was rewarded. Together with others she has been involved in its revitalization:

After we came back here, all the Loucheaux Bibles were worn out, gone. We had no more Bibles.

I was sure I could get more hymn books from Old Crow or in the Yukon. They use our language all over. They use the same books as we use. Although they have a different accent, we still understand them.

I felt very bad about not having Loucheaux Bibles and hymn books. James and I talked about it and decided to have a meeting to tell them what we thought they should do. The old people told us, "Look here. We are the ones who do the Loucheaux service and after we are gone, there will be no more Loucheaux. It's no use wasting time on the language, and besides that, there's no money for the books, no more money."

That was why they hadn't got any more.

In 1976, the Canadian Bible Society republished the Loucheaux Bible prepared by McDonald.

I had to spend a long time praying. After two winters, a young professor came from the States. Right away, of course, my husband always takes people in. Maybe they're travelling, maybe they want tea, he said. In this way, we meet people and get to know them. When he met this young man, he told him to come. He had tea with us and told us why he was here, he wanted to learn the language.

It was 1957 or '58. Twice a week he'd come and we'd teach him our language, through tapes, talking into tapes. That winter he stayed but he had a hard time, he had no money, nothing much to do. He got stories from old people, people helped him, but we were the regular ones. And one day, he said he couldn't make it here.

He said he'd try the Yukon. So, he wrote a letter. They told him to come over. He went over, and then he wrote back to me and said that right away he went to the Yukon Bishop who gave him his promise that he was going to help him with Loucheaux.

Then he got a grant from the government. So, when I could, I sang into tape the Loucheaux hymns, read the prayer book, and read the Bible. My husband was teaching him language. Then my husband got sick.

He moved to Whitehorse, this young man. He started working, but he kept sending tapes and [called to] talk to me on the phone and remind us of this and that. The next time he came back, he talked just as good as me, sometimes even better than me. So this has been 16, 17 years and I read the Loucheaux Bible into tape so people can hear it. I'm reading Jeremiah, which is very hard in my language.

I have two more chapters. I have read, one by one, on my own, the whole Bible in my own language. It took me nearly two years, slowly, you know, from Genesis to Revelation.

Over a hundred years ago our Bible was written for us and it was never changed. It was written in the old Loucheaux language and there are young people today who don't understand it. It is hard on the young people, because they don't understand.

Now, my language is being written down in three different dialects. Each one is a little different. A woman from Arctic Red was a translator in early days for Archdeacon McDonald and wrote in our own language. Another woman over the mountain was married to a Hudson's Bay man and she learned to talk English; [she] talked her language as well and was a translator for a minister. And here, too, there was a woman who talked her own language and was a translator as well.

I read the way I talk, the way we talk here.

This young professor, phoned me and he told me that everybody, everyone in the meeting wanted to say hello to me and they were really thankful. He said that they listened to my tape and they wanted to thank me. He said he talked Loucheaux really good because of auntie. He calls me his auntie. He said, "Auntie, your reading is getting better and better. It's so perfect and while you're still at it, I'd like you to do some more."

So I said that you keep me alive by doing that. I still like to do something for the church.

The name of the young man Sarah saw as the answer to her prayer was John Ritter, now attached to interpretive services in

Whitehorse. A genius for languages, he is full of admiration for the people, and has done much to further the recovery of the language. Ritter has produced a different and simpler orthography to write Gwich'in that is now more commonly used than McDonald's, including in the schools. Ritter has used Sarah as a language consultant in his work. Her extraordinary memory has assisted in other ways.

When my husband was working in Old Crow, in charge of Old Crow, I worked through the church records. I looked after the books for him. In that way, I knew about old names. When people get stuck to find the background of someone and don't remember people's names for the old age pension, I happen to know. And then I wrote down some things that I wanted to remember. I worked hard to remember things like that because I helped my husband with the church. At baptisms, I wrote everything down for him. I helped him know the background in all these things. This is the only way I knew, and through my grandmother.

As an elder, Sarah is asked now for advice. Although unsure at times how to respond, her usual response is one of love. She has a particular concern for the young who are growing in communities that are quite devastated:

I have just turned 89 now [in 1990]. Since I was very young, I have known the missionaries because I went to their school and my grandmother was a very prayerful Christian woman. She taught me prayers and she said that I had to go to church.

Sometimes I think I haven't had an easy life when I was growing up, but still, I've lived well so far. Now, my first adopted girl, my daughter looks after me really good. She calls and says, "Mama, how are you?" Sometimes, I don't feel right and sometimes she comes over. All my adopted children see me as their own mother. They live all in town. Many people check on me all the time.

We're trying hard to bring the young people back into the church. I talk to my young people sometimes. They come to me and they say, "Grandmother, I am bad."

"Who says you are bad? Who knows you are bad? Nobody knows who is bad," I tell them. "You're good. I'm sure there's something good in you, yet. Use that."

"Thank you, grandmother," they say.

This is the way I talk to my children, my young people. Only through love will we bring them back. I talk to my friends sometimes when they ask me. I don't know if I'm right or not, but this is how I feel about that. I don't want to tell them that they're doing wrong, that they're no good. I don't do that.

Whatever you ask the young people to do, if you do it with them, they'll all come and work together good. But, if you ask them "Be like this" and, "Do this!"—no.

One little hymn that the Native people did for themselves is:

Come to Jesus, Come to Jesus, Come to Jesus, right now.
Come to Christ, Come to Christ, Come to Christ, right now
He'll save you, he'll save you, he'll save you—now.
You need him, you need him, you need him, you need him, right now.
I need him, I need him, I need him, right now.
Alleluia, Alleluia, Alleluia, right now.

All the children in the Yukon, Indian and White, sing this one. It is one of the hymns made by the Indians, and it is nice.

Sarah still remembers the old times vividly:

One time my husband and I one time went to Old Crow by dog-team through Rat River travelling slowly. When we got there, we spent a week there. Then we started back trying to make it back here for Easter. It took us 10 days to come back. Now, I went over to Old Crow. It took me one hour. And, again, I think I am a real old timer. When I went over to Old Crow by dog-team, I saw all the country. Many things I didn't know, I saw—like the name of the mountains and the creeks that I hadn't seen before—I hadn't known them before. I know them now, I remember them. But, now, I just fly right over them, I don't see anything.

The mountains all have their names in Loucheaux. Everything has its own name. I once tried to explain to someone what the lakes mean, every lake has its own name. "What does this mean?" he would say. I would tell him. "Thank you, thank you!" he said. "Come back again," I said, "I am one of the only old timers left!"

It may seem to Sarah that she sees little, but she sees it in ways that many never will. She carries an understanding of a culture that many, even among her own people, will never experience. Among leaders of church and government, she is a legend in her time. Until she was in her nineties, she lived summers at her home in McPherson Village, returning winters to live in Yellowknife with her daughter. Her daughter worried, but Sarah said, "I prefer staying on my own." Sarah now lives in the seniors' home in McPherson. Her daughter continues to press for her to live in Yellowknife, but Sarah is strong-minded, and resists the idea. She has been quite ill recently. In her illness, she has vivid dreams, a gift of the spirituality of her people. On two occasions, she has seen her husband, James, who died some years ago, "But he was turned sideways, not looking at me, and so I know it's not my time yet," she said.

The Arctic is a place of strong contrast, particularly in the quality of light. The winter is long and dark, with occasional bursts of the magnificent aurora borealis dancing across the heavens. In long Arctic summers, there are several weeks of midnight sun with almost no darkness. Late afternoon and evening soften into pinking shades of light stretching over vast space. The terrain seems empty at first, but looking closely, one sees grasses, shrubs, and small flowers blooming everywhere, clinging in every crevice, the sky awash above in colour, shades of subtle colour. A southern eye has to look carefully, to pay close attention to see this delicate beauty.

And there is the sparkle, the bright twinkle in the eyes of a gracious elder in a land thought to be barren. From her dreams Sarah knows that she is not yet ready to go. One day, in her dream, her husband will come again to see her, and he will be looking straight at her, and she will leave us to go into that even greater light...

Dr. Jessie Prettyshield Saulteaux

Recorded and edited by Joyce Carlson

Jessie Prettyshield was born on August 22, 1912, at Carry the Kettle First Nation to Elizabeth Good Elk of the Assiniboine Nation. Elizabeth's mother, Ocapeoda, was an Assiniboine medicine woman. From Ocapeoda, Jessie learned about the Assiniboine world view that honours the sacredness of all life:

My grandmother was 96 when she died. One of the things she told us was if we needed anything, for example, to cut a tree for firewood or any other useful purpose, we were to cut only what we needed. Now, when we know and understand that leaves absorb waste from the air, we understand this better. But, how did she know and understand this?

When we were children, we were great ones for breaking branches when we were out picking berries. To my grandmother and to the elders, everything was sacred. They had respect for everything. When digging roots, she would first take tobacco and place it where the root was. Then she would take what she needed off the top or root and place the rest back in the earth and cover it up. She would always put back what was not needed.

Each tribe kept its own camp. When the head man or chief went out hunting, they were only to take what they needed and not to waste anything. In that time, we were told always to share. I remember both my grandmother and my father saying, "Even if you are hungry, if you know someone else needs something, share what you have."

They always said Great Spirit when speaking of God, and they always said that they were to look after this land for the Great Spirit.

For 200 years, the Assiniboine inhabited a vast western plain that spanned the border of what is now Canada and the United States. Jessie's family refer to themselves as 'Nakota.' The Assiniboine are part of the Siouan language group and lived to the east and north of their Siouan cousins, the Lakota and Dakota, and to the south of the Cree and Ojibwa peoples of the Algonquian language group whose territories extended from Lake Superior, north to Hudson Bay, and west to the Saskatchewan River. Assiniboine territory had extended more to the east, from Lake Superior to south of Lakes Winnipeg and Manitoba before the onset of the fur trade around 1640.

With the establishment of the North West Company in Montreal, the Assiniboine became customers of Ojibwa middlemen to the east. When the Hudson's Bay Company began operating from the north, they travelled to northern posts instead and became middlemen to western tribes, the Blackfoot, and to their Siouan cousins to the south.

During the fur trade, Assiniboine peoples formed diplomatic relationships with the Cree, initiating a mutually beneficial alliance. They continued their seasonal movements following the food cycles, using European trade goods to their advantage.

A hunting and gathering people, their pattern was to winter in wooded parklands of central and western Manitoba and move out into the plains in spring and summer. The buffalo hunt provided their staple food. They were skilled hunters; berries and wild fruit and herbs grew in abundance. Summer was a time of gathering for festivals, Sundances, and social events. The Assiniboine were a welcoming people, open to people travelling in their country.

After a century of trade, the Assiniboine, along with their Cree allies, extended their hunting grounds to the north and west. They dominated the fur trade and controlled much of the great western plain from "The Forks," where the Assiniboine River meets the Red River at Winnipeg, to the southern tip of Alberta, just west of Cypress Hills, south to the Upper Missouri and north to the Saskatchewan River. In 1833 their population was estimated to be 3,000 tents (or lodges), each comprising a family of four or five.

As the fur trade spread farther inland, their role as middlemen lessened and they adapted by providing food, especially pemmican (dried buffalo mixed with wild fruit and berries) to the many trading posts along river systems throughout the northwest.

At the height of the fur trade era the Assiniboine had been living in an area estimated to be some 20,000 square miles in a vast plain with wooded areas along rivers, and many marshes and lakes with ample fresh water. Winters were severe. Their understanding of the country, hunting skill, and ability to make shelter, and fine, warm clothing, particularly with buffalo skin, enabled their survival. They controlled a vast territory while maintaining economic autonomy. Their social structure was upheld by their spiritual and cultural traditions.

In my grandmother's time, they always prayed to the Great Spirit to look after them. I have sometimes wondered how it was that they knew there was someone, some being looking after them, someone they could pray to. Where did that knowledge come from? Who was the Great Spirit who came to them?

But they knew it. In our tradition there is a special blanket called the star quilt. Hand made of beautiful colours, it is made by the women for their sons and husbands and brothers. It is patterned after the morning star. Just before the first light of dawn there is a star in the east, as the colours of the new day begin to spread in the sky. It is said that it is the brightest of all stars. This star most represents the Great Spirit, shining through the darkness, greeting the first light.

When the men were going away, the women prepared a feast, inviting all to come, and they gave the guests a star quilt to honour their men. When the men returned there was a feast and celebration. If they didn't return, there was a feast to share the sorrow, to mark the time and to honour the ones who were gone.

I think sometimes of the star, the morning star, how in the early days they used to make the star quilt for the men and how they saw everything as sacred.

A particularly sacred place for the Assiniboine were the Cypress Hills. Rising out of the plains at the western rim of territory that had been theirs for centuries, the hills were lush, with rich plant and animal life, beautiful hills, valleys, and freshwater streams, an oasis in the great plain. When the buffalo began to recede from other parts of the plain, they were still to be found at Cypress Hills. When other game also began disappearing, Jessie's ancestors settled in semi-permanent villages in this area, the most fertile and only mountainous area in their vast territory.

The increasing scarcity of game together with a number of other factors outside their control combined in the early to mid-1800s to create serious difficulties for the Assiniboine. The North West Company and the Hudson's Bay Company amalgamated. Before the amalgamation, their fierce competition had created a dependence on the Assiniboine and Cree for provisions. Traders were unhappy with their great dependence on the Assiniboine. They saw the self-reliance and economic autonomy of the Assiniboine as arrogant.

The establishment of the Red River Settlement with an increasing Métis population undermined the role of the Assiniboine in supplying provisions to posts. Even then, the Assiniboine remained confident of their abilities to adapt until they were struck by epidemics. Assiniboine peoples had lived intimately with the land and knew about many natural medicines. Jessie's grandmother had a particular gift of healing:

My grandmother knew about medicines. She said that in all things there were both good and bad; she told us about the good—but she never told us about the bad.

There were medicines for earaches and toothaches and for pains anywhere. There were medicines for birth control and for miscarriages and there were only certain people in each community who knew about the medicines; many people used to go to her for the medicines.

In 1817–18 they were struck by a whooping cough epidemic, followed by an even more devastating smallpox epidemic in 1837–38 when they lost over half their people. These European epidemics to which they had no immunity created terrible hardship. The people who remained were but a remnant of the Nation. Their own medicines could not help them, and smallpox in particular inflicted terrible suffering.

At the same time, the scarcity of game created increased competition for the few remaining good hunting grounds. Territorial boundaries were no longer respected. Skirmishes and wars were increasingly common between Assiniboine people and their Cree, Blackfoot, and Sioux neighbours. The Cypress Hills were regularly visited and camped in by other bands. Posts had been set up by both Canadian and American traders anxious to profit from the many tribes hunting there.

Liquor was an illegal trade good in both United States and Canadian law, but American traders working north of the border in Cypress Hills traded in liquor knowing American troops could not enforce their laws in Canada and Canada was not yet able to enforce its own laws. [The North-West Mounted Police were not founded until 1873.]

The stage was set for conflict. In the winter of 1872–73, many bands were camped close together. Liquor was freely flowing. A number of Blackfoot and Cree camps were close to the Assiniboine in Cypress Hills when a band of European wolf hunters, people who hunted with strychnine poison and sold the pelts for bounty, arrived. Historians have suggested that these hunters, in a highly drunken state, accused an Assiniboine of stealing a horse. A Métis trader warned the Assiniboine of the hostility of the wolfers, whose anger appeared to be fuelled by animosity to some of the other tribes camping in the Hills. Jessie describes the rules of their camp as her grandmother told her:

In the tradition of the Assiniboine, there were certain rules and ways of the camp. She told of the travelling, how the men used to travel in the front and the women at the back. This was so the men could protect the women and children if they were attacked. The men and the women had their different duties and they knew and understood the different duties they had.

When warned of the threat, Assiniboine men were sending the women and children of the camp to safety while they stayed at camp to deal with the hunters when the hunters came upon them. Jessie explains how her grandmother was stabbed.

The first name of my grandmother Ocapeoda in the Assiniboine language is translated in English as 'stabbed many times.' Her last name has the meaning 'Good Elk.' Here is how she received her name.

When she was 14 she had a dream. She dreamed that she was attacked and stabbed. In her dream she was told what must be done to bring healing to her wounds. She told this dream to her people. Years later, the dream saved her life.

One day, when she had left the camp with the women and the men were guarding the camp some distance away, she was attacked. My grandmother fought. She ran up the side of the hill and when she was running she threw snow back to try to slow the man following her and cause him to fall. This made the man very angry and when he caught her, in his rage he stabbed her again and again. He stabbed her 13 times. She was found unconscious by her people and taken to a tent where the medicine people administered the healing in the way she herself had seen in her dream. And so it was that in her dream she had prepared them to know how to treat her wounds. She was so badly stabbed that her lungs protruded from her body. I saw her scars from the wounds when I was little, and I felt them on her body.

Nineteen Assiniboine men were shot and another was clubbed to death. The severed head of the clubbed man was placed on a pole outside the trading post. In the drunken debacle that followed, five Assiniboine women were captured and raped. While some of the persons responsible were brought to trial, all were acquitted. This incident has been described as "unbridled barbarity" and stands out as the most brutal confrontation between white and Aboriginal people in western Canadian history.

The North-West Mounted Police were sent west by the autumn of 1873 to aid in keeping peace, but the suffering of the Assiniboine continued. By 1879, the buffalo, their staple food and shelter, had been hunted to extinction even in the Cypress Hills, their last retreat. In the 1870s the Canadian government formed treaties with all First Nations. The Assiniboine were one of three bands that at first refused to take treaty. In the massive starvation that followed the disappearance of their livelihood, the Assiniboine took treaty on September 25, 1877, in exchange for food rations.

In 1880, Jessie's ancestors were forced to move from Cypress Hills. Jessie's grandmother Ocapeoda travelled by foot with other Assiniboine peoples hundreds of miles to southeastern Saskatchewan near Indian Head.

In my grandmother's time in the Cypress Hills, we were already under the government. They were saying that because it was crowded, they wished to give us another spot. It was then that the people were brought to Carry the Kettle Reserve. It was so named after a chief whose name was Carry the Kettle. The first name of the reserve was Take the Coat after Chief Take the

Coat. When Chief Take the Coat died, it was called the "Assiniboine." Recently it has been renamed "Carry the Kettle." When the people first came, they found they did not like it. In the first winter, there was much hardship and quite a few deaths. When spring came, the people returned on foot to the Cypress Hills which was their home. They liked it so much better there...in the hills, and it was the place they knew. But then, they were brought back again on flat train box cars, forced to come back to Carry the Kettle. This time they were given the oxen and plow and the farm inspector to help them get started into farming.

This was in the winter of 1881. Starving and threatened with imprisonment, the people who had once dominated all the prairies were now settled on small reserves. Jessie's ancestors finally agreed to stay on their reserve south of Indian Head. Some were hopeful at first about farming, believing that if Europeans who seemed so "helpless," and knew the land so little, could find their livelihood in this way, then surely they who knew the country so well could succeed. The reserve was very small, however.

In the settling of reserves, members of the same family were scattered. Jessie's stepfather, George Prettyshield, was known to be a deeply spiritual man from a strong family. Two of his brothers, Lean Man and Mosquito, both became chiefs of their own reserves. While it may have been common in the past for members of the same family to become chiefs, distances and government laws requiring permits to travel broke down family and social relationships. All affairs were governed by Indian agents appointed by the government. Jessie describes the impact of this on the people.

Up to the 1940s we really couldn't travel anywhere. If you wanted to go anywhere, to go off the reserve for any reason, to see anyone, or to visit, you had to get a permit. There were lots of reasons for going off the reserve, but you always needed a permit. Also, if anyone wanted to come to the reserve, they needed a permit as well. The longest one could stay anywhere, even with a permit, was a month.

This was a time of upheaval and massive resettlement. At first, three reserves were settled, very close together; later, one reserve moved, and the other two amalgamated. Disputes about the land continue to this day.

During the formation of the reserve, peoples from different cultural backgrounds joined the reserve. A woman from Ochapowace, called Travelling Woman, of Saulteaux First Nation had been born near Broadview, Saskatchewan. She had married and moved to Montana. When mistreated, her husband's people suggested she return to her own band. She was journeying back to her own people with her two young boys when she encountered the Assiniboine in Cypress Hills and journeyed with them back to Carry the Kettle. She became a member of the band, and married there. David Saulteaux Senior, Jessie's future father-in-law, was the second son of Travelling Woman. He married Bella Blackface from the Birdtail Reserve in Manitoba where her people had sought refuge after the massacres of Dakota peoples in America. Jessie married David, Jr., the son of David, Sr. and Bella Blackface. Because they were different, the family were referred to as that "Saulteaux" family, and the name stuck.

With social disorganization on a small land base, persons of different ancestry were sometimes ostracized. David Saulteaux, whose name itself set him apart, experienced some ostracism. The pain of this created a deep commitment to welcome the stranger in the Saulteaux family.

The Birth of Jessie

Elizabeth Good Elk, Jessie Prettyshield's mother, was born in 1876, three years after her mother had been brutally stabbed in the massacre. She was four during the forced move to Carry the Kettle.

Although the Nation had experienced enormous change, they were firmly rooted in their culture. Elizabeth Good Elk was married according to the Assiniboine custom to George Prettyshield, a much older man, when she was a young teenager.

Marriages of young teenage women were often arranged with a skilled older man, a good hunter. Once a young woman had proven herself, had gained skills essential to living, and had perhaps given birth to children, she would be eligible to choose a much younger man as a husband. The later commitment would often be made in her late twenties.

In her relationship to George Prettyshield, Elizabeth gave birth to four children. Later, she formed a relationship with Joseph Jack, a younger man who was a cousin of George Prettyshield. Joseph Jack was also the son of Chief Take the Coat. At that time, the Assiniboine had had hereditary chiefs. However, Joseph Jack had been only eight years old when his father died, and so his uncle Carry the Kettle assumed leadership.

The four children Elizabeth Good Elk had with George Prettyshield were grown and having their own children by the time she formed a relationship with Joseph Jack. George Prettyshield, by this time a very old man, told her not to forget her older children and that his home was still her home. When Elizabeth had four more children with Joseph Jack, George Prettyshield cared for those children as his own.

Jessie, the second child of Elizabeth Good Elk and Joseph Jack, always considered George Prettyshield her father. Elders have often remarked on the amiability of their parents and grandparents towards the marriage relationship. It wasn't uncommon for more than one wife to live together with one husband, or for a woman to have more than one husband. Skilled hunters who were able providers might well have more than one wife. Chiefs often had more than one wife.

Jessie's children, Bernice and Frank, recall visiting Joseph Jack throughout their childhood. They now recall with some amusement that he showed a special and extraordinary interest in all of them. At the time, they didn't understand why the man they believed to be their uncle showed such tender care. It was not until they were grown that they understood that Joseph Jack was their birth grandfather. Jessie herself referred to him as her uncle. His real identity may have been hidden because, as with other Assiniboine cultural and spiritual traditions, their parents were aware that the family might be harshly judged for following the Assiniboine marriage and relationship customs. The Government of Canada had banned the practice of Native spiritual traditions. During the late 1800s and early 1900s, missionaries had come to convert the people to Christianity. Missionaries and other European newcomers had different understandings about marriage and relationships. Jessie's parents were anxious to adapt to new ways, and tried to help their children make this transition.

I remember when I was very young that my brothers and I were playing on the farm, and high up in a granary, suspended from a rafter we found a rattle, drum, and medicine bag along with a pipe and sweetgrass. We were playing with this and my father came and found us. He told us we were not to play with this—that the missionaries had told us not to use this—and he had put it away. He told us we were never to use it and he hid it. He must have hidden it good because we never saw it again.

My father must have been a medicine person when I think of it now. But both my mother and my father accepted Christian ways. They thought that this was best.

Jessie's grandmother Ocapeoda never converted. She remained an Assiniboine medicine woman until her death in the late 1920s. Jessie was born in 1912, seven years after Saskatchewan became a province of Canada, a time when the memory of the old ways formed an important part of community life. From Ocapeoda, Jessie learned about spiritual traditions of the Assiniboine culture.

My grandmother, my mother's mother, never put away these things. She kept her medicine bag, her pipe, and her sweetgrass. I remember being with her when she would go out and dig her medicines, her seneca root for earache and other ones, one for vitamins and iron, and one for depression. If a person lost a relative, they could take a medicine to help them with that. There was a medicine if one were working too hard—or if one had problems with the heart.

While Sundances had been banned, attendance at social gatherings, ceremonies, and pow-wows was more acceptable. Jessie has a clear memory of those events:

I remember going with my grandmother to her Indian ceremonies. There were different ones who would give advice and tell others what to do. Also, there were ceremonies where different ones would seem to go into a trance—and I remember when I was small that I was scared. I reached for my grandmother and hid under her shawl! There were some who used to speak in tongues like they sometimes do at gospel meetings in some Christian churches.

While she went with her grandmother to Assiniboine ceremonies, she also went with her parents to the Christian church where her mother was becoming a leader:

I remember that the first time we were going to church on Carry the Kettle, there was nothing but a shack, a small shack without even inside walls. The minister made a fire very early to warm it enough for us to come. Then, a stone house was built early in the 1900s. The missionary started the Women's Missionary Society and my mother was made the president. The secretary-treasurer was the missionary's wife. We used to have picnics. We made quilts and aprons and pillowcases. Many of the early pictures of the Women's Missionary Society were lost in a fire.

When the first missionaries came, Catholics had their own Indian groups—and when you went there, you had to have a feather pinned in your hair; often, one sang songs that seemed to be warlike gospel songs. Then, the Presbyterians also had meetings—and I remember the people going to that and it used to be that some people went into a trance. If they were sitting down, they might fall in the circle and they might faint.

It was always good to go to those kind of gatherings because they always had lots of lunch after. It was a gathering of the people.

As Jessie grew, she was touched by a Christian teaching:

The first missionaries in the community were Mr. and Mrs. McKenzie. He got sick and died and she stayed on for about a year. She used to go and visit in homes and had started the women's society. They talked English in services, and I didn't understand the words. One boy who came back from school interpreted for us, and he'd go to Sunday school and show us the pictures, telling us about the pictures.

When I saw the pictures, I really understood what they were talking about when they talked of Jesus. There was a picture of Jesus as a shepherd holding the lambs in his arms; there was another with Jesus with the little children. I have thought of those pictures many times. They have always stayed in my mind.

Jessie was always very close as well to her grandmother Ocapeoda, who was in her seventies at the time Jessie was born. One of Jessie's strong memories is of her grandmother at prayer:

I remember my grandmother best with her arms upraised in prayer. Once there was a storm coming, a great storm, and my grandmother went out to meet it. She stood before the storm with her arms held high and she prayed to divide the storm.

I was a child then. It seemed to me as I watched, that it happened just this way, that the storm was divided by her prayer.

The continuing relationship with her grandmother informed her Christian faith all of her life. This relationship to her grandmother became even more important when tragedy struck. There were storms that even a medicine woman simply could not prevent.

My mother had tuberculosis when I was young. Then, when she was expecting a baby again when I was 12, she died of a heart attack. It was just too much for her. That's when her heart gave out.

I remember although I was young, only 12, on the evening that she died, there was supposed to be a pow-wow. When the people at the Young Men's Christian Association hall learned that she had died, they quit their pow-wow and most came to the house. [The YMCA had been an early mission to Carry the Kettle. Jessie has always spoken very highly of this mission endeavour, which strongly encouraged leadership in the community.]

I saw them standing in a circle in front of the house in starlight outside in the night—and late at night—between 12 and 2 in the morning, they suddenly stopped talking and it seemed as though the northern lights came closer and closer and reached down to where we were. The beginning of the northern lights seemed to come right down and it was as though one could be carried on the light—and the men seemed to be following it south because they heard voices singing a pow-wow song.

I always remember that, how it happened that way that the northern lights came to our house that night.

My mother was 42 when she died.

The death of Elizabeth Good Elk was a deep blow; her early death precipitated more change in Jessie's life.

People were sent to school according to need. Because I had lost my mother, I was sent away to residential school. My father thought that since we had no mother, it would be better for us to go to school because he didn't feel he could teach us the things we needed to know. The minister that was there came to talk to us—and he thought it was best for us to go and there was a place for us at Round Lake. My father talked also to the farm instructor and he also thought it better for me to be away since I had no mother.

When I went to Round Lake, I was 12 years old and I didn't know a word of English and didn't know how to get along in English. I stayed there until I passed grade 8.

I had a young sister and a young brother. My sister went away to school with me; my brother stayed and went to day school on the reserve. He died of dysentery when he was 12 years old.

When a family loses a mother, the children seem to lose contact with each other and are not close to each other any more; I don't think it would have been the same if we had lost our father. I felt that if I had had my mother I could have talked to her, I could have told her things. With my father, it wasn't the same.

I have always felt that those who have their mother long are lucky.

A natural leader, Jessie did well in school.

I went to CGIT [Canadian Girls in Training] and to mission band and to Sunday school. It seemed always I would become president of one or another of these groups. Here, I got experience about leadership. Here, I also got to know a girl from grade 8 who wanted to go into nursing, and they got her to go to St. Boniface. But she had to go in as a French girl because they didn't accept Indians at that time.

When I finished grade 8, I couldn't go back to Round Lake School. They told me if I wanted to stay I could work in the school laundry. If I wanted to continue school, I could go on to another school. They told me to go home and think about it over the holiday. I thought about this and decided to go to Brandon. I wanted to take nursing and thought this would be a way to go into it. But, I got sick before I finished grade 9. I was 18 then.

The school had sheep, and the sheep were killed for meat. I was not used to the meat of the sheep and they gave us the grease from sheep instead of butter on our bread. The principal arranged for me to take separate food and it helped. They didn't expect me to take exams, but I did take the exams. I passed, although I never went back. By that time I found out that I was too much of an Indian; I was too dark to be accepted into nursing.

I wanted first to go to school to be a nurse. That was what I really wanted. But, when I could not do that, I did not want to come back to the reserve. It was only when I knew I wasn't going to be accepted in training or in a job, I came back to the reserve.

I have learned much later that there is land there in the Cypress Hills which still belongs to the Assiniboine. I heard so much about it, how beautiful it was there. If I had known that when I finished school, I would have gone there; I didn't want to come back to the reserve. There was nothing for me here. If I had known of this other land, I would have liked to have gone to the Cypress Hills.

While away at school, Jessie received another blow.

When my grandmother died, I was far from home at Round Lake School. They sent word that she died, but I wasn't able to be at her funeral. I really wanted to be there. The death of my grandmother was hard to take. When my grandmother died, I couldn't be home. I always remember how I wanted to be home, how I longed to be home at that time.

With both her mother and grandmother gone, and the door to further education closed, Jessie returned and made the best of her situation on the reserve.

With two brothers and my sister and the other young people my age, I tried to see what we could do on the reserve. We had basket socials and dances. We had hockey games and skating wherever there was a good slough; whatever we could round up and organize, we did.

In those days, the YMCA was quite strong on the reserve and they trained local leadership. Around 1925 to 1932 they came to the reserve and they had a few meetings with the men. From then, the men carried on and they used to take turns holding services. At that time, too, they had a minister who used to come once a month. The minister did the marriages, but even for funerals, the men trained in this way by the YMCA took the services. Later on, when the other denominations took over, the YMCA and the local leadership died off.

In the midst of the massive and enforced changes, there began to be drinking on the reserve. The elders cautioned Jessie:

They used to warn us of alcohol. They used to say "Stay away from firewater." In those days, there was little liquor on the reserve. The only way that it could be brought in was if there was a white man buying hay, or cowhides, or furs. Some always came with liquor but until I was a young woman, I saw very little of it. There were sometimes a few who used to sneak what they could outside at the dances—but very few. There wasn't much liquor around that I remember until after I left school in the thirties. Only two or three on the whole reserve used to carry on with liquor.

At home, I lived by what I saw others doing. My older sister got married, and I saw her having to do housework. I learned how to do housework as well. There were certain ways that we were taught as girls. We were taught what we could and couldn't do—we weren't even to lift our skirts a tiny bit when in front of boys, even our own brothers. This was the teaching of our tradition. Today, everything is different.

Early in the fall, just after returning from school to the reserve, Jessie was sought for marriage. This first attempt to match her didn't meet with her approval.

It was 1932 when I left Brandon and I married the following spring. A man came with a team of fine horses and offered the team to my father if I would marry him. I told my father that even if he was the last man on earth, I would not marry that man!

Jessie's birth father, Joseph Jack, whom she referred to as "cousin Joe," then became involved in marriage arrangements that were more successful.

My future husband then started to visit. He came a few times. I really didn't know what he had in mind. Then my cousin Joe came and said he thought I should marry. I think I was open to this because I had seen him a few times over the fall, and so when this was suggested, I was open to it. There was someone else I was going with. I thought more about him. I don't know why it happened that way. Maybe it was for the best.

In the Assiniboine language there are certain ways to talk about people, and certain ways of describing relationships. If one was related to a person, the relationship was described in the language and so if a person whom one was to respect made a suggestion, then one felt one had to do what was suggested. This is the way it was when I married. Cousin Joe said this was a good thing to do. There are words that show respect—and these words then tell you how you are to treat that person and from which persons you would take advice.

Jessie married David Saulteaux on April 28, 1933. David, grandson of Travelling Woman, had lost his first wife in 1932. She died of tuberculosis, leaving him with an infant. David was 22 when he married Jessie. Jessie cared for the young child, who died just few months after their marriage, also of tuberculosis.

At my wedding, I made my own dress. Different ones gave us a little and we had a few things we needed from our father. Usually we got help with what we needed.

The things I needed to know, getting married, getting children, how to look after a home, we learned from my grandmother and later my sister helped me.

My sister was a good help to me and we lived close together. When our husbands were away and we needed food for our children, we sometimes set snares for rabbits, and we set snares for rabbits in the fall when they were fat. Sometimes we could go to our mother-in-law for help. My sister did a lot to help when there were problems, although she had her own problems. She was beaten often. I don't know why he did that.

Jessie continued with her Christian faith; her husband practised Dakota spiritual traditions:

When our family were young, we saw that they were baptized. Sometimes it was two weeks and sometimes it was a month after they were born, but we saw to it that they were baptized before they were grown up although they only had church services once a month. Sometimes the student ministers came to us from May to September, and when they came, they always seemed to come to me for advice on what they were supposed to do. Many times I had my own problems but I always had a way to get over them knowing that God, that Christ will carry the load. Christ will carry the problems. I believe that when we pray and ask Christ to take our load, he does. I don't think, though, that prayer is answered right away. It is strange, sometimes, the way that prayer is answered.

Through discipline, I have always had respect for anyone older. I always felt I had to listen to those who were my elders. My father was very good to me. After I had my second baby, he used to come and visit me, from that time on. In the old days, it didn't matter how old someone was, everyone always tried to do as much as they could. They always tried to make their own firewood. Even today, they try to do the same. I think that this is a good thing, to work as long as you can at whatever you are able to do.

David Saulteaux supported the Christian teachings of Jessie, although his own spiritual life was guided by Dakota spiritual understandings, similar to the Assiniboine traditions of Ocapeoda, Jessie's grandmother. These traditions had begun to re-emerge in the late twenties:

Just before I left school, the principal's wife took us to a camp, and whoever wanted did bead work. Perhaps they realized that we were losing our own culture and they were trying to bring it back. In those days, we were not allowed to speak our own Indian language. We couldn't have pow-wow dances or Sundances. When they started the first Sundances, they had to have them out of the way and back in the bush.

I was in Round Lake School when the first one happened and after that, different ones had Sundances. At that first one, the leader was said to have the power to heal. They brought a little boy and it was said that he was just skin and bones and when they prayed for him, the leader said he was going to grow up, but that was all that he would say. The child did grow up, but was killed when he was a soldier in the Second World War.

Many Assiniboine people served Canada in both world wars. David Saulteaux had applied to join the army at the beginning of the Second World War, but was not accepted because of poor health. His older brother joined, returning after the war with a bride from Europe.

As a young mother, Jessie continued to practise her skills, utilizing whatever materials were at hand, and learning new skills in gardening and making preserves.

I've always liked sewing. When the children were little, they always wore what was made over. The Indian Agent used to give us old army surplus things to work with. I remember that when I had two young children, I made a beautiful suit for the boy and a skirt and jacket for the girl. Others made quilts. We had a way of making quilts so that we put our names on them. We called them friendship quilts.

The Indian Agent asked if he could send two quilts and the outfits I had made for my children to Ottawa, just to let them see what we were doing. He told us that we would have these things returned to us. We never did see them again, although he did give us more materials so we could make more.

During the summer, when the berries were ripening, there were opportunities to go to the school and can berries. There was a person there who showed us how to do canning. Whatever we picked, we could put up in the basement of the school. This was during the summer holidays. I liked also to make jelly from the berries. If you are making jelly from the cherries, you need to make it in the first week that it's ripening, otherwise, it doesn't gel as well. Pin cherries make the best jelly. Sometimes people would give us some crab apples and they make a good jelly also. Sauce could also be made of this and we found we would make it very well and it was good.

For the last two years I have been unable to tighten the jars and so I have had to give up canning and jelly-making.

Jessie took on more and more responsibility. She was called on to help with sick people and in difficult times with her community.

Over the years, I was a midwife, and I helped when the babies were born and tended to the sick and people came to me to dress the bodies when they died. I remember going to my mother-in-law's house where the sister of my husband, a girl of about 18, was dying. When we got there the girl told her mother to give us lunch and she was okay. After we finished lunch, she called her mother and said, "I'm going to sleep now, mom." And she closed her eyes and took her last breath. The house was so small I wasn't far away. I had to wash her face and change her clothes for the wake and funeral. At that time they used to make their own box and line it with blankets and a pillow.

The increasing breakdown in the community caused by alcoholism now began to affect Jessie's sister's marriage, and her own.

Today, wherever you go, wherever you turn around, there ar*e* people drinking. I didn't know what to do. When it first started to happen, I talked to the minister and to the farm instructor, too. They didn't seem to be any help. The minister said I might go to the owner of the hotel and tell him about it, and he would put a person on the blacklist. I would have to have a good reason to do this.

I don't know what he meant by this. Did it mean if a man is neglecting his family or beating his wife or family? There were many who did beat their wives when liquor was open to Indians. I was not beaten. Around the time that I would be putting children to bed there would be visitors [drinking]. There was one room in the house and on one side of the room were the visitors; on the other side of the room I was reading Bible stories and Sunday school papers to the children as I was putting them to bed.

The liquor he [David] would get from white friends who would come with favours. But the children always had food.

It is strange how a man, when drinking, will sometimes laugh and cry—and pray. He was a hard worker and a good gardener. At that time groceries were cheap and he was generous with his garden and with his working for others. He won many prizes for gardening. He often gave money, but it was hard to talk to him about many things, especially about alcohol—what it was doing to his mind and to his body.

Attempts to talk didn't help, and David became increasingly dependent on alcohol. His children relate that David worked steadily all week, and always ensured that the family had enough to eat before buying liquor.

Since David had experienced some rejection because of the differentness of his background, he and Jessie were always welcoming and hospitable. Many of their friends were Cree and Métis. They helped David's brother and his wife, a war bride. Although very connected to their own traditions, they spoke English in the presence of peoples of differing cultures so as not to exclude anyone. Jessie knew the many good points of her husband and attempted to be positive:

He got some good teaching, although there was no one to say the kinds of things that my grandmother taught us. I remember his father holding our oldest daughter when she was only three and saying "This is a precious child of God in your home, and you must look after her. When you have a child like this, be good to her and don't treat her rough because she is sacred. She must learn how to look after her own life."

This which his father taught is the same as he now teaches with his own grandchildren.

Every now and then I remember him giving that advice to his own boys. He also told them it's hard to go through life. You're going to meet bad times, bad friends, don't fight or hold a grudge. When that happens, if someone should hit on one side of the face, show them the other side of your face. Don't fight. He also said to always remember they have a home.

The breakdown in the community affected every family. The children, in attempting to understand David, affirmed the importance of "home" for their father. He was a generous man, and both parents were hospitable. In addition to the five brothers and sisters, they also had many others staying with them. Jessie's sister was beaten many times. Afraid for her life, she finally left, and Jessie and David cared for four nieces and nephews. Other adults and children stayed from time to time. Travellers to the community, often strangers, were welcomed. Even wounded animals and birds were brought into the home, cared for until they were able to fend for themselves.

David's lifelong struggle with alcohol placed a strain on the family. Bernice and Frank reflect that he was unable to talk about what troubled him. Like Jessie, David had been sent to residential school, an experience he described very late in his life to his children in little bits. Others who knew him from school said he was known most for the frequency with which he ran away from school. Returns were accompanied by brutal beatings. He had two particularly painful memories of the school; one was of a young boy working in the barn who was trampled by horses. Another was of a boy forced by older children to ride on a wild horse, and whose neck was broken when the horse bucked. Other memories appear to have been blocked.

David did continue the practice of his spiritual traditions, and he was respected for his contributions. He served his community as gravedigger, saying, sometimes the only way to help people is at their death. In spite of the ostracism in his community because of his differentness, he was a gentle man.

Although he had received a lot of criticism, elders looked more to him as spiritual traditions were honoured once again. He had a special role in caring for the sacred fire, smudging the food for feasts, and looking after the sacred pipes. In plains Nations where peoples moved frequently, the role of firekeeper was extremely important. He earned the respect of many through his integrity in organizing and serving at feasts and special events.

He participated in the recovery of cultural traditions well before Canadian law permitted this, practising traditions separate from the Indian Agent. The Sundance was an important rite of all Siouan peoples, including the Assiniboine, and he was given Sundance songs by the elders, songs he kept until his death. Jessie accepted his gifts, and supported him by being present and cooking at the ceremonies although she didn't take part.

In the late fifties, when the Sundance and other ceremonies were allowed again under Canadian law, David had many of the honoured jobs, including working with the elders at cutting the logs for Sundance poles and placing them, as well as serving as firekeeper.

It was painful that members of the church itself had also said the Sundance was wrong. He had also prepared the church for services by going early to light the fire until told once by a minister that he was a drunkard and shouldn't be there. David stayed away from attending church, although he did help in practical ways whenever he was able, such as in cleaning the yard.

Jessie was not critical of David's return to traditional ways as her own childhood had included some understanding of this:

I learned about serving and leadership in school. But, I remember it was a man's job in the Indian way to serve and handle the sweetgrass and smudging the pipe with sweetgrass in a ceremony. In a ceremony, everyone sat in a circle, and when they started a meeting, they began by following the sun in the circle. This meant that there was a place for everyone. This did not mean that they *had* to talk. It was so that each person felt that there was a place for them, and if they wished to speak they were invited to speak and felt they had a place in the circle.

When I was a child, if there was a ceremonial feast, they didn't allow the children even to stand up. They all had to be still. Up to 1938, every gathering I went to in my community was in a circle. Another thing was that the men sat together on one side of the circle, and the women on the other with children as well. I think that this helped in keeping a sense of the community. Now, everyone sits in family groups. I wonder whether this contributes to the breakup of the community, and of the families as well. In my time we used to visit a lot; now it happens seldom.

Jessie respected what she found helpful in the traditions of her grandmother and of David. Her own spiritual life was guided by those understandings, as well as by Christian teachings, particularly two key passages:

I was talking not long ago to someone who said he had nothing to live for. I said, "It is God who put the breath in you. It is Jesus who calls you earnestly and tenderly, and I will pray for you." I've been through a lot and I still think that the best thing is to remember 1 Corinthians 13.

If I speak in the tongues of mortals and of angels, but do not have love, I am a noisy gong or a clanging cymbal. And if I have prophetic powers, and understand all mysteries and all knowledge, and if I have all faith, so as to remove mountains, but do not have love, I am nothing. If I give away all my possessions, and if I hand over my body so that I may boast, but do not have love, I gain nothing.

Love is patient; love is kind; love is not envious or boastful or arrogant or rude. It does not insist on its own way; it is not irritable or resentful; it does not rejoice in wrongdoing, but rejoices with the truth. It bears all things, believes all things, hopes all things, endures all things.

Love never ends. But as for prophesies, they will come to an end; as for tongues, they will cease; as for knowledge, it will come to an end. For we know only in part, and we prophesy only in part, but when the complete comes, the partial will come to an end. When I was a child, I spoke like a child, I thought like a child, I reasoned like a child; when I became an adult, I put an end to childish ways. For now we see in a mirror, dimly, but then we will see face to face. Now I know only in part; then I will know fully, even as I have been fully known.

And now faith, hope, and love abide, these three; and the greatest of these is love.

1 Corinthians 13:1–13

Jessie describes how she applied the learnings:

There was a potato patch on the reserve. It was a patch that everyone worked on. Each person had their own place in it, but you weren't supposed to pick any potatoes until a certain time in August. I remember once talking to my brother-in-law. It was after a rain and there was not much to eat on the reserve. My brother-in-law said that he thought he would go to the potato patch and get some potatoes; it was soon enough for the potatoes, but we weren't supposed to pick them until the farm inspector said so. He said, "I can pick them in the night, and with the rain washing away the tracks, no one is going to catch me!"

I remembered that all my life. It wasn't the potatoes, whether someone would catch him at that. That didn't really matter and I can't remember if he got caught stealing his own potatoes, but I remember telling him, "There's someone watching over us. Someone is sure to be seeing us in everything we do, in every part of our lives."

The 23rd Psalm and 1 Corinthians 13 are what I have really lived with. I have met a lot of different people in different ways. Sometimes people talk about others in bad ways. But there is something in the verses which is very strong and which tells us of the love we should have for one another. Even if people talk about me, I couldn't hate them. These passages and all the other little passages I learned when a child have really helped me through life.

The LORD is my shepherd I shall not want.
He makes me lie down in green pastures;
he leads me beside still waters;
he restores my soul.
He leads me in right paths for his name's sake.
Even though I walk through the darkest valley, I fear no evil
for you are with me;
your rod and your staff—they comfort me.
You prepare a table before me in the presence of my enemies;
you anoint my head with oil; my cup overflows.
Surely goodness and mercy shall follow me
all the days of my life,
and I shall dwell in the house of the LORD
my whole life long."

Psalm 23

Those who knew Jessie recall that she was one who always showed respect in relationships:

I always talked to people who were farm inspectors and agents and teachers with the title Mr., Mrs., or Miss. This is a sign of respect.

I was the janitor at the school. I was with the boys and went to clean the school. The farm instructor came with the mail and a cheque. Then, a man came to talk to the farm instructor—and he later said that he had caught me with the farm instructor. He was meaning that I had done something wrong. I explained that this was not true—and my boys were with me in the classroom and so there was no doubt that this was not true. I explained that I have always called the man by his last name. I did not call him by his first name. This was because I respected him.

Jessie and her husband, David, worked hard in a variety of jobs on the reserve, looking after horses and cattle, as well as continuing to care for others.

After my children grew up and finished school, they all went their separate ways. Then we moved off the reserve to Wolseley. My husband got a job on the tracks with the CPR [Canadian Pacific Railway] during that winter and I did some babysitting and housekeeping. In the spring I got a housecleaning job out on the farm but it turned out to be a permanent job for almost 10 years. My husband and my oldest son worked there until 1969. We moved back to the reserve and I became a chief in the next election.

During that time our United Church minister asked if I would work as a lay minister because there just seemed to be no one they could find to come. So, I told him I would think about it because I felt so small. Anyway, later on, it came to my mind that it was a calling from God. I knew He would be there to help me so I told the minister I would try my best.

I had to take care of the church happenings like baptisms, weddings, and funerals. Anytime one of those things would happen, I would call to my supervisor and he would come and hold those special services. For my part, with no education, it wasn't easy.

I was paid about $300 a month. My supervisor said to get together once a week to plan a service, and so I would go on my own and do what I could about holding a service. And I did the visiting. When I wasn't able to walk to the people's homes, I got my daughter-in-law to drive me.

I held wake services and the minister held funerals. He would do the main part, and I would read the scriptures and I led in the singing. I did this then for about two years. Then there began to be criticism. Some people began to say, "Who is she to be doing services like this?"

I knew I didn't live a perfect life to be a church worker, and I always asked in my prayers for God to forgive me. I knew God worked and that He forgave me so I thought I could do a little. This is why I did my best to get the Indian Ministers program going. People saw me as a sinner and thought I shouldn't do the service. They thought of the white ordained minister as a perfect person and they looked up to him.

It is discouraging to try to help God and to be criticized and this still happens. When this happens to the ministers of our own people, I say to read the scriptures and don't listen to gossip. Even in the Bible, Paul persecuted the Christians and later God came to him. Don't give up.

The thing that spoiled everything was liquor coming in. We had a good United Church Women's group going and when liquor came, one by one they all left. I don't know why, but everyone was scared of being president. I think this will improve now with the help of youth leaders.

Bernice, my daughter who is now the minister, is in many activities and she is trying to get cultural awareness groups going. She started with a young group of 10 to 12 and now she has a group of 16 young people. They try to get to know about their culture, about the Sundances and pow-wows. It is something like a Sunday school class.

The minister asked many years ago, in the fifties, if I would go to Prairie Christian Training Centre to attend courses, and I did. My husband was willing to look after the children, and Bernice was just starting in school then. We were caretakers at the school then. I was glad that my husband was always willing to look after the children and without complaint.

Jessie was the first woman in Saskatchewan ever to be elected chief. She was supported by her husband in her work in the church, and began to be called on more and more for counselling. She had an increasing role as elder, one who is able to provide others with wisdom in learning how to live. Increasingly, she integrated teachings of Assiniboine and Christian teachings:

I try to make my children understand that they have to teach their children what is right. Until they finish school, they have to learn how to live. After they finish school, they have to make their own way. As they go, they will be meeting many bad habits. When they get to be around 30 or so, they have many difficulties, then there is the time things change. They are either on the bad way—or the right way. They have their own children by then—and they have a big job as parents.

From 40 on there is another period when, if they have children, it's their job to teach them the right way.

I still remember in school, in science study, there was a picture of the earth and you could see it, the many layers of the earth being cut. Like that picture of the earth is how life is. There are many layers and stages, different levels of earth and soil and rock and each has their own place. Life is the same as that. In the time from our fifties to seventies, there is also a time of helping others to know how to live their lives. When I look back on my own life I find too that I see what I came through. What it reflects, too, is where the earth was cut. I find too that having the spiritual life has helped me from giving up.

With all the bad things I have met, I couldn't keep on living if it had not been for God, always being there, always willing to take me back as one of his children.

I have been asked to speak at the Alcoholics Anonymous a few times. They asked me what I thought. I told them that God has created everything. God has put us above the animals and given us the earth to look after; I told them to think of these things, and look after their spirits and their bodies. Always to think that what they have to look after is not theirs, it is God's. Everything is sacred. For that reason, they must look after themselves. They must never break a tree, or damage even a stone. Above all, they must always try to find the talent that God has given them and try to carry it out.

I have had people come back to me later and thank me. I was glad to know that they had grasped what it was that I was trying to say to them about these things.

The idea of finding one's talent was important to Jessie. She understood that all needed to find their gifts. She had lived through deep sorrow in her own life, had experienced deep pain, and had found strength in God's word. She knew that people needed to be raised up from within their own communities to be trained in a way appropriate to their cultural understanding. She knew from her own experience that new leadership would need to affirm their own cultural traditions to bring healing. She knew that there was a kind of denominationalism in communities that caused great pain.

I think now there are too many denominations. The Y was good; they trained the local leadership. We had hymns in our own language with them. They were really active in those days when I was in Round Lake School.

Sometimes it troubles me that there are so many visions and versions of the Bible, and some of what happens in prayer meetings and services isn't right; it doesn't give me a good feeling.

Some of the understandings of some of the Christian denominations, I just can't accept or go along with. It is strange how it seemed the same in both the Indian way and in some of the Christian ways. The early Church Missionary Society and YMCA people seemed to have a good way to my thinking. It is a shame that those kinds of training and local leadership were lost over the years.

She was discerning, and sometimes critical of the many denominations who came to her reserve. Yet, she respected that others might be helpful at times, and welcomed their help:

One time, my son was drinking and parted with his wife. I didn't know what to do. I told him to remember that it is God's life that he is looking after when he is looking after his life. Then I said a prayer in my mind to God to send help. Half an hour later the Mormons came. They talked to him and stayed for quite a while. I told them he needed help. I said, "I'm alone and don't know what to do." They stayed and talked until he was better.

Rooted and strengthened by both Aboriginal and Christian teachings, Jessie took what was helpful from each, and encouraged her children to find their own ways:

With my own children, I think it is important that they make their own decisions, that they have their own choices, especially when it comes to who they should marry. Someone came to me and asked me whether his son could marry my daughter. And I said to him, "It is up to her, what she wants to do alone. It is her life and you will have to speak to her."

I always remember going to Arizona in the 1960s with a minister. We heard a warning about war. We stopped and we wondered what to do. Then his small child said "There's going to be no war; we must trust God." We went ahead, and there was no war at the time. Children often are able to call us to understand and trust. Is this why we call children sacred and holy?

Jessie had a special place in her heart for children. She yearned for all to develop their own leadership and potential. Like her grandmother's prayer that divided the prairie storm, Dr. Jessie has in her life divided many storms. Her leadership followed after the strength of her grandmother and other women in traditional teachings. The Great Spirit of Assiniboine traditions and understandings of Christ were deeply connected:

I have sometimes wondered how it was that in my grandmother's time, they knew there was someone, some being looking after them. But they knew it. It is said that it is the brightest of all stars. This star most represents the Great Holy Spirit, shining through the darkness, greeting the first light.

I think of how they saw everything as sacred.

Sometimes when I see the morning star and it seems to be so very bright, I don't feel surprised that the people saw this star as representing God. It is so bright just in the earliest hours of the day, just before the new day as soft light begins to light the sky and touch the earth.

That is God. That is God being there for us. The Great Holy Spirit with us.

The elders always said Great Spirit when speaking of God, and they always said that they were to look after this land for the Great Spirit. Which of the tribes of Israel are we from? Which of the tribes of Abraham are we? We are surely one of those. I suppose it really doesn't matter since we are all children of Adam.

Jessie loved learning. She studied the stories of the Bible, trying always to apply them to her own life. She also understood that generations of oppression and differing cultural understandings made learning in a European style difficult. Many had had negative experiences of school through the residential school system. People even experienced racism at theological colleges.

In 1983 Jessie was awarded an honorary doctorate from St. Andrews College, a United Church theological centre, for her outstanding contributions to The United Church of Canada. She continued to work tirelessly with others in the early eighties to establish a centre for training Aboriginal leaders. The Centre was opened in 1984 at a ceremony in Fort Qu'Appelle, Saskatchewan, 45 kilometres from her home in Sintaluta, Saskatchewan.

At the time of the opening of the training centre for Native theological students, I was standing at the ceremony, and it seemed to me that I saw a clear light around the people in the ceremony. I was expecting that they might ask me to speak, but they didn't. And then later on I saw many little lights and I think that those lights are like many little stars and those lights are the lights of our young people as they begin to take training and become leaders in our communities.

At the time of the ceremony, I didn't say anything, but I hoped that over time, we would find that we were doing the right thing, by finding ways to bring leadership training to our own people. A few times, it just about seemed to fall apart. A few times, it seemed that people were saying we shouldn't be trying to do this on our own, we shouldn't be trying to do our own training.

We have to be guided by someone. So, with the help of our ministers, we have come this far and we are going into a brighter future. All those little stars are going to get bigger, they are going to shine brighter. There are going to be more and more leaders.

I remember and think about my brother-in-law and his two or three rows of potatoes and I think of someone looking after us. His saying, nobody will ever see me, nobody will ever know.

Someone will always see you, someone will always know what you're doing. God is always there to know what you're doing. I remember the first pictures I saw in Sunday school. There was a picture of Christ with all the little children. Then there was another with him again, being a shepherd. Those pictures were important although we didn't speak English. By looking at those pictures, we knew what they meant. After going to school, I knew the words to the pictures. But the pictures alone were enough to understand.

The training centre was named The Dr. Jessie Saulteaux Resource Centre to honour her contributions and leadership in its development. Jessie continued to trust God. In the mid- to late eighties, while she was in her seventies, she travelled to meetings across Canada, was involved in discussions around the Apology to Native Peoples in 1986 and the formation of the All Native Circle Conference in 1988. She continued in her work as elder with the Dr. Jessie Saulteaux Resource Centre, the All Native Circle Conference, and the Saskatchewan Treaty Women's Association until a year before her death in 1995 at the age of 83. She died just a few months after the death of her husband of 62 years.

Jessie Saulteaux was quiet spoken, a humble person who respected others, and entirely non-confrontational. She carried an authority in her own person. Both gentle and strong, she walked with a cane and she walked carefully, measuring each step. Her voice was rich, yet soft.

Jessie's decisions were guided by wisdom and discernment. She understood that her people needed to see themselves in a positive light; for this to happen, they needed to be open to First Nations cultural traditions. In her lifetime, some of the traditions began to re-emerge even more strongly:

Some of the old ways are coming back. Now, when we have a feast, a ceremony, or after a funeral, we sometimes have a pipe ceremony. All are invited to participate in these ceremonies, both men and women.

At times, my grandmother used to tell us to look after ourselves, respect ourselves, and not to fool around with the boys or men. I didn't know what she meant about looking after one's body. A person is free to look after one's own body and has no one to blame but themselves if they don't.

We are set free to do whatever we want now in the matter of our own ways. A lot of things that happened in the Old Testament, like the sacrifice of animals and how they bled, how they carried the ark of the covenant, were changed. To me, this resembles the sacred bundle. They have now in the All Native Circle Conference the freedom to do all these things. If they want to carry on the Indian culture, they are free to carry on in this way. But, for me, going to boarding school, and having my father say what he said about putting away the sacred bundle, I think he must have been a medicine man, I don't know what to say.

My father put away his bundles and his medicines. In our Bible studies not long ago we were told in the Old Testament they used to burn offerings and carried the sacred ark of the covenant. When Christ came he told us that he was bringing new commands; all the old laws of the Old Testament were gone.

I think we should look at it in this way. Both are good. I've heard men talk about the white man's religion being the Bible, cross, and holy water; and the sweetgrass, pipe, and ceremonies are the Indian way. The Indian way has nothing written down. We learn about their wisdom through their talking.

When I have attended a ceremony at my daughter's with my husband, I have found that it is good to be there. My husband has said after hearing those Sundance songs that he really felt good. Many people my age go now to the ceremonies and they say that it is good and we should have those things every now and then.

Through Jessie, many who had negated their cultural traditions began now to affirm those traditions, and understand their importance for the next generations. Jessie was a healer, always searching ways to help others. She understood God's love in her life; it gave her a wonderful lightness of spirit, a quality of joy. It was clear that she held in her heart the image of Jesus as caring shepherd. This was profoundly connected to the morning star, which was for her the great Holy Spirit with us.

Those of us who were privileged to know her felt the power of the great Holy Spirit through her. It was a truth she carried within herself, within her own spirit. For the hundreds of people at her funeral, the power of the Holy Spirit was present in the outpouring of grief, in the sharing, in the feast, and in the reconciliation that happened in her community. It was even present in the symbols and imagery, both Christian and traditional, that intertwined at her wake and funeral.

Her honour song at her funeral feast was hauntingly beautiful. At the beat of the drum, one could feel her spirit rising joyfully, dancing lightly, embraced by the great Holy Spirit. Her body was laid to rest on a hillside on a cold spring day. Those who knew her remain warm in their memories of her.

Jessie's legacy continues. The Dr. Jessie Saulteaux Resource Centre is a unique learning centre where the culture of First Nations leaders is affirmed while they study ministry. Most return to serve their own communities. The vision continues in the living out of the traditions in her family. Her son Roy cared for his parents until their death. Daughters Marita and Aletha, excellent seamstresses, share the image of the morning star in quiltmaking. Her daughter Bernice, one of the first graduates of the Centre, serves the United Church in Carry the Kettle. Son Frank graduated from the Centre in the spring of 1997.

Gladys McCue Taylor

Edited by Alf Dumont

Gladys McCue Taylor was born in 1914 in a small house overlooking Buckhorn Lake in Curve Lake First Nation.

The reserve, close to Peterborough, Ontario, was first formed in 1827 when scattered people from several Nations settled in the area after the wars between French and British. First Nations peoples had been recruited to join those armies. The Huron had been almost completely wiped out by the wars. Their remnant in Southern Ontario joined with others and moved to the Curve Lake area.

This community was steeped in the ancient traditions of the Anishinawbe [known for many years as Ojibwa]. It is surrounded by water yet close to major cities and European communities. Gladys' family are rooted in closeness to their traditions, while living in a continual relationship with the outside world. Gladys became a bridge-builder, able to live and walk in two worlds. She lived in the tension between cultures, and the continual struggle to reconcile the two brought a deep well of living water, a stream that has given rich gifts to her home community, to local First Nations, to the All Native Circle Conference, and to the larger church.

Gladys was a drummer. She was active in pow-wows and sang in the local choir. In her early school years, Gladys was punished for speaking her language. Fiercely proud, she refused to allow that to deter her and continued to speak the language and in later years taught it to others. She always spoke and prayed in her own language in church. She received many awards. The Curve Lake First Nation had a celebration day in 1992 to recognize her for being one of Curve Lake's "firsts"—the first Native woman minister. In 1991, she won a Senior Achievement Award for being the first and only Native person to be granted a certificate from The United Church of Canada to give a communion in Ojibwa.

I have journeyed with Gladys Taylor for a number of years. She has shared many stories and teachings with me. She also shared many moments of unresolved internal struggles.

Her story is told here through a collection of her writings from several sources. They are the stories she told me, the jottings she made on scraps of paper she found in hotel rooms or in margins of business agendas, and excerpts from her well-crafted, eloquent speeches. From this collection we can recognize that Gladys, like many elders whom we respect and from whom we learn, was on a long, long journey. Not all of her thoughts were complete. She shared wisdom from her journeys and from her life stories only after she had wrestled with her thoughts for many years.

I met Gladys Taylor in 1980 when I was involved in the coordination of the National Native Consultations for The United Church of Canada. As a planning group, we sent out invitations to church elders and leaders in the First Nations communities, where the United Church had a historical connection. Curve Lake was one of those communities. Gladys was one of the honoured and respected elders in that church and in that community. She was asked represent her community along with another respected elder, Murray Whetung.

The first consultation, of 11, was held in Wabimasquah (White Bear Reserve, Saskatchewan) at their summer camp. We gathered to share stories of spiritual development in our communities and in our lives. Gladys in her own quiet and compelling ways became one of the elders many of us would consult.

Gladys, with her good friend Murray Whetung, became the first Leading Elders of the All Native Circle Conference in the United Church in 1988. Gladys helped the community that was forming understand the role of "elder" as listener and advisor to help others find their own way.

Later a gathering of Cree elders from Northern Manitoba, led by Johnston Garrioch and Moses Wood, told the gathering:

We as elders are not here to tell you what to do. We offer the wisdom of our experience and then leave it to you to make the decisions as leaders. We will be watching you to see how you act wisely. We will be watching you.

Under the watchful eyes of the elders, a community of faith, a community of spiritual people, matures. Often, we are given the privilege to journey through life with profound teachers. Sometimes we are given the responsibility to share their lives and their teachings with those who come after, who have not met them.

Elders share with those of us who are younger because they know that we want guidance. They hear the pain in our hearts. It hurts their hearts. Their wisdom does not come easily. Gladys felt that she could give wise counsel only after years of thought and prayer and sharing with other elders.

Elders do not like to be pressured. Their answer of silence is a teaching in itself. Often they want us to slow down and walk slowly so that we can hear each other's hearts. We need to be quiet and listen for guidance from the spirit.

On April 2, 1993, Gladys wrote these words for Bailley, a special child she loved, and to all of us who became her children:

Child of two cultures, you are rich. You travel through your two different worlds, learning all the best and good ways of each. As you drift in and out, your mind will always be your guide. Little one, as you travel in your canoe, take a lesson from your craft. It may be slow, but it is sure. There will be time to dream, to choose, and to take hold.

Many of us remember Gladys as an actor on television as Riel's grandmother or as a grandmother and elder in the *Spirit Bay* series. Many of us remember the stories she shared with us around camp fires or in the many lodges she visited. The stories that she shared with us were often humorous ones, like the time, in the still of the night after many hours of partying and dancing, she returned home and climbed into her husband's long johns while he was still in them, thinking in her momentary lack of lucidity that she was just crawling under the covers and having a difficult time. There were colourful stories she never wrote down. Those stories will always remain with us.

This chapter reflects an elder's wisdom that comes from some of the stories she shared as she looked back on her own life and saw that she did not walk alone, but walked with the spirit of the Creator.

*Bizindan Weweni**

I would like to share important parts of my life. I will start from the day I came into this life. In those times all babies

*A glossary of the Ojibwa words used in this chapter is on page 100.

were born at home. I was born in the year 1914, on the third day of April. [Richard, her husband, died on the same day, April 3, in 1977.] Mom told me years after, I was born with a veil. Her midwife, whose name was Mary Jacobs, but everyone called her Shognoshqua, brought a lot of babies into our community. She told Mom, because this baby was born wearing this veil, she will be of use to her people. Now 71 years later, I got my licence to bring communion to my Indian people. This is how far into the future our people could see. Little did I know their dreams were coming true, when I took up my work for native ministry.

Gladys, that gentle Ojibwa teacher, knew the importance of cross-cultural sharing. Throughout her life she had worked hard to transform attitudes that divided people. She never forced her thoughts on others but led them by example and with gentle teachings.

Fifty-six years after her marriage, Gladys stood at the window of her home, which was only a few steps from the house of her childhood memories, and began to reflect on her life. She wrote these words that August day.

At dusk as I look toward the purple and gold sunset, my mind travels far, to the day, when we stood side by side and took our vows till death do us part. Now I stand alone and look at the beauty of the ending of another day. The wisps of white hair crown my aged face but my mind still remembers the good times, also the hard times. It's 56 years today, since I called you my own and that's the way it will be till I come to join you. I always walked behind you, or waited for you. But some day this will come to pass.

There are times in life when the mind is keen to reclaim precious memories. Gladys recalled these words from her youth that celebrate the richness that comes from honouring the Creator in two spiritual traditions:

THE FISH STORY

Long ago, when I was a young girl, when we would see or hear tell of an old person [who] went for a swim, we would say, now all we will do, is go and pick up some fish that will die, after the old person was through swimming. We were only fooling of course. That time has come true for me in my old age. Yesterday evening, me and my girls went for a swim. The water felt so good, I didn't want to get out. So the girls came up to the house, along with Pete. But I stayed just enjoying the water. As I stood there, I could see something swimming on the top of the water.

I waited. Then to my surprise, it was a fish. I made a couple of grabs for it and caught it with my bare hands. And I made a dash for the dock. And I called Pete as hard as I could. They all came running down, they thought something was wrong with me. But I was holding my fish down, all out of puff. It weighed about 10 pounds. I cleaned it and got 24 pieces from it and put it in my freezer for next winter.

Granddaughter

Granddaughter as I sit by my window facing the lake, memories of yesteryear come to keep me company. There's so much to remember. Our joys as we seen the return of spring, the ice break, how it made music along the shore as it came around the point at the old house. No musical things on earth can be made to compare to it, because it is the sound of the Creator, letting us know He cares for us. Now you're all grown up and on your own. I'm glad life has a lot to offer but you must choose wisely for life isn't all that long, that we can waste time feeling sorry for ourselves.

I Had a Doll

When I was a small girl, I had a doll, a baby doll. I loved it very much. I kept it for a long time. I would look at him and imagine in my childish way, that some day he would grow up strong and handsome. Each day my love for my doll grew. I used to talk Indian to him, teach him our way of living and I could tell just by looking at him he was proud of his heritage, for I could almost hear him say, "Someday, you are going to be proud of me." Till one evening I forgot him outside. It rained that night. Some time coming on morning, I thought of my doll. I went and asked pa to go and look for him for me. He mumbled, "Go back to sleep, you probably put him where he wouldn't get hurt." But my heart ached so much. I got brave and went to look. There was my doll, soaking wet. Someone had run over him. His head was broke. His leg too. His arm was partly torn off. So when I picked him up, his sawdust poured out, making him look so limp and pitiful looking. I took it home to show pa. I think he understood how bad my heart was breaking, because my tears were like twin rivers pouring out of my eyes and united at my quivering chin.

Pa said, Your tears will be the evening star, for the evening star as it sets, disappears beyond the hills, but will reappear three times: two tears for my eyes, and one at my chin. That is why it always comes up. My three tears for my little boy doll.

I am an Old Woman now, an Indian grandmother. You can be stripped of everything you own but memories stay forever.

When I Was a Small Girl

When I was a small girl, I remember being taught by both my parents to have great respect for our church. They said it was the house of God, a Creator who was able to see all the world with all the people in it, for He had made everything that had life, that meant people, animals, birds, fishes, trees, grasses, the world with the sun and moon, stars, a canopy of living nature, where we were all able to talk to God, as we do to our fellow man every day, because he was only a breath away. But on Sunday we always went to Sunday school then to church. Mom always cleaned up the house on Saturday and cooked most of our Sunday meals then she just warmed things on Sundays. She always said, "This is the day of rest. We aren't suppose to do any work." You never saw a canoe on the lake all day. Of course there were not any cars in those times on the reserve. People just stayed home or went to visit neighbours and elders. I used to like this because they always told stories.

Then coming on dark we always went home. Most of the times Mom didn't light the lamp. We would go straight to bed. We would name all the Mary's or the Tom's or we would count all the widows and bachelors. Just when we thought we named them all, we'd remember another. After a while we would fall asleep and it always seemed the night was so short it was time to get up.

We had our work we had to do before we went playing. There was wood to bring in and put behind the stove and kindling to split up fine and brought in and the reservoir in the stove had to be filled, along with the two water pails. Between the chore time and the play time we went to make beds and empty the pot. We took turns at this job. Because our mattresses were from straw or corn husks they had to be ruffled up.

On cold frosty nights, when the frost would hit the house Mom always said, "Mr. Jack Frost is mad tonight, he wants to come in. If you go to sleep he will think we're not home and go away." We didn't each have our own bed. Mom would go and get coats and put them over us and we would put on our stockings, sometimes our toques to keep warm. We never had fire all night.

In the morning you could see your breath. We used to put our fingers in our mouths and when the cold hit, it would steam, making it look like a stove pipe, and we'd say, "I made fire already." But there was hardly any sickness.

Those days, the snow was so deep it hid the rail fences. Big snow banks, where we could play. We would take the shovel and take some snow out of the snow banks and make a house. We always wore rag moccasins and Mom would make warm stockings out of sweater sleeves; then there were the insoles she used to make. I just wish you could have seen them. They were two long pieces of cloth sewn round at the toe and then the two long pieces were wound round the ankles. They were very nice to wear, because the snow couldn't get into your moccasins. They called them *tush-kunun*.

I guess people could say that we were poor. But we were happy and warm. And we knew the winter wouldn't be too long. Those were carefree days. They were so good. No worry. So much freedom. It was so good to be young and alive.

One night I couldn't sleep. I went downstairs to get a drink of water; besides, I had to go to the toilet out back. The stars seemed to be extra large and bright and there were so many. When we were going back to the house I asked my Dad why do the stars come out only at nights. "Well the sun is a stronger light. It outshines all the other lights."

"Are the holes in the sky the reason it rains?" I asked.

He smiled so kindly, and said, "No. Those golden holes aren't for the rain. It says in the Bible if we are good and kind to everyone, when we die we will go to the Golden City where even the roads are gold and God put those stars there so we will remember when we look up to the sky, we are going there someday."

So I said, "What about the ones that are bad, they look up there too."

He said, "Everyone gets a chance to turn over a new leaf, because God doesn't want anyone to be left out. God is love."

I often think of Dad and feel I was so lucky to have a father like him. For he taught me a lot: things that are worth remembering.

SUMMER'S HEAT

I'd like to share a story about what happened when I was a small girl about five years old. My parents were very hard working people. They put in a big garden. We picked berries in the summer. Mom made pickles. And Dad gathered black rice, in August, if he wasn't guiding. He made axe handles in the winter. Many times he'd walk to Peterborough with his hand sleigh packed with handles, which he would barter with the farmers for pork, also some knitted mitts and socks from the farmers' wives. We never wanted for food. That's when the seed of spiritual belief was planted in my young life.

I remember this one time when it was a very dry summer. We had to bring water from the lake to water the garden, twice a day. This time Mom was tilling the potatoes. The dust was just rising with each stroke of her hoe. Her sweat was just pouring down her face, along with the dust. She looked so pitiful. I wanted to help her, my sister and I. But she said, "No. It is too hot for you. Sit in the shade." She worked on, until we noticed her. She was standing with her forehead on top of her hands, where she held the handle of the hoe. We thought she was sick. We started to cry—softly. We were afraid she'd know. She stood for a long time. I ran to her after she started working again. There were tear tracks through the dust on her face. I asked her, "Mom, what's wrong?"

She looked at me in the wise way she often looked at us. Then she said, "I'm so tired, but I know that I have to keep on. Dad isn't home, so we have to keep working." Dad was guiding at a place called Fees Landing in Omemee. She said, "I asked God to help us. We must believe that he will." So coming on dark, she took us down to the lake for more water and to wash up before we went to bed. We had a lunch, then we lay down on the floor. It was hot, so we couldn't sleep. We heard Dad call outside. He had come home. Mom was very glad. He came in and we got up to get Dad to kiss us. We went back to lay down.

They talked. Then we heard them pray before they went to bed. All was quiet. We fell asleep, until I woke up to hear Dad saying, "Get the girls up, I hear a storm coming." We got up. Dad always smoked to the thunder. He would light up his pipe. Pass it to Mom. She would pass it to my older sister. She'd pass it on to me. This is a ritual of the Indian people. Then the storm broke. It really rained. Then both went out. With flashes of lightning, we could see them holding each other, with their heads bowed in thankful prayer. It rained off and on all night, on through the day. Then we were having breakfast. Dad gave thanks for food, home, family, and for the rain they had asked for. So I asked him, "Did God really answer your prayer?" He said, "Yes. It says in God's Book: 'Whatsoever you ask in his name believing that's what he will do.'" The seeds of spiritual belief were planted in my early youth and through the years until now, I trust in Him to supply all my needs. I just walk by faith and He will do the rest.

Memories bring deep feelings to the surface. Gladys was not afraid to share that part of herself. Acknowledging these feelings brought her healing, and brought us the important teaching that we need to share all our feelings to discover our wholeness:

It is Saturday October 24, Mom's birthday. Nothing can measure my loneliness today. [Gladys' mother died in 1978.]

Acknowledging her feelings and exploring them led to dreams that guided Gladys to know herself at all levels. All the elders acknowledge and teach that we must first come to know ourselves. Knowing ourselves and accepting our journey, we then can help others as they journey towards the land of the spirit.

BLEACHERS

[In one dream,] I was sitting beside the bleachers feeling very lost and friendless, when a big black car came toward me, blowing its horn. I moved out of the way and as I looked at the people in it, I seen chief get out and walk toward me. He folded me to his breast with tears streaming down his face. He said, "Mom, it's nice to see you."

He was sick looking and his clothes didn't fit. But he was clean. He had a blue windbreaker. In the pocket was a hair ornament, a baby's face. It held a nice white feather. He said, "Mom, it's for your hair." And there was also a small bottle of something that looked like sand coloured seeds. As we talked he said, "Mom, I come for you. You'll come live with me. Granma came to live with me. Let's go see her." We went. She was busy cleaning her little house. She had made a birch bark flower pot and it wasn't finished yet. I felt so happy. The chief said, "Let's go." I said, "Don't leave yet." "Well I came after you Mom. I'll have to go now." I turned to speak to Mom. She wasn't there. The only thing I seen was two figures flying toward the east. I can feel my hopes and heart crumble. I called out, "Wait Chief. I'll go." But they just kept on going. I woke up crying.

Incidents involving concern for others can often take us back in memory to those we have always held dear. Later that day she wrote:

He knew that I didn't want him to go as evening came and the night took over. My fears for his safety as he crossed the ice were more than I could bear. I cried. The tears on my face were hot. I had looked on the lake too long. I prayed,

"Dear God if he don't come back, please take him home to the other side of the lake."

Someday, when cold tears run out of those weary eyes, it will be too late to come back. Just memories of mother and a name they will soon forget.

Honouring Mom

It has been a few years since you have gone. But you always seem so close. You taught me all the good things and useful things, I know. And if I have any good ways in me, you gave them to me.

Having a mother is the most precious treasure a person can ever own. All other treasures can be replaced but a mother's love is one of a kind, next to the love of God. It is the next to this.

She sought to honour her mother, because as a mother she knew the pain of all mothers who at one time or another are forgotten by their children and grandchildren. This was something she tried to teach all those who became her children. Gladys also acknowledged the difficulty of all mothers to remember what their mothers and grandmothers taught them and to honour all the teachings they received from all the spiritual traditions they carried inside them.

Big Silver Bird

I hear you pass but you're gone beyond sight. If I could confront you face to face, I would ask you where did you take my grandson. My loneliness comes and goes like the faint breeze of summer that shakes the grasses and ripples the lake. I recall the day he came home to us. No baby was ever so sweet. He looked older than most newborns.

The Rhythm with Which My People Sing

Frosted window panes, the banging of Jack Frost on the tin tarpaper covered walls. The whistling of the north wind through the gaps of the cracks on the corners of the house. The rocking chair has found its way to the creaky floor board on the floor. The singing of the tea kettle on the stove top. As I sing to my little one, snuggled close to my breast, I often wondered what rhythm my people follow as they sing, slow and softly. It has come like the sure sign of spring refreshing with promise as I sing, as I rock in my chair. Now I know it's the rhythm.

My Roots...My Children's Roots

This day is overcast and my outlook is just as grey and dreary as the day itself. My heart ache from last evening still hangs on. Those days come often now. It makes me wonder if it is any use trying to fit into the white world of my children. My roots are very obvious. My ways, my thinking, even my looks. I'm just as unique as an arrowhead.

Changes of the Years

When I was a child times were so different. There was no rush to get things done. There was always time for everything. No noise. We went to bed when the darkness came and got up when the sun was coming up. There was no need for lighting the coal oil lamp. Only when it was storming, when poppa would get up and hang quilts over our windows and put another over the stove. He would take the looking glass and turn it to face the wall. Then he would fill his pipe and we would all go downstairs. He would pass the pipe to Mom. She would hand it to my sister. I always got the stronger drag, because I was the last. We always did this. Even yet I have my pipe ready to make peace with the thunders.

As I stand at my open window, I remember the times long ago. We could hear the echo when we would call. Now my friend *pswawa* must have moved away, because I never hear it anymore. I remember hearing someone pounding a black ash log to make baskets or splitting wood before the day got too hot. As I would sit beside the lake you would hear the fish splashing around, or the throaty croak of a bull frog, or someone making rhythm with paddle and water. The smooth waves of it passed along the side of the canoe. Away on the other side the loon is heard as it lifts its call to shatter the surface of the lake that was holding like a mirror. The waking breeze ripples along the water lily's bed. The weather bug says it is going to be a hot day.

I hear a car start up. Its horn blaring trying to wake someone to go to work. Then a motorboat takes up the chorus. Someone is trying to sing but just can't hit the tune, so they just yell. And I bet they'll get a gold record! Crazy Crazy Folks!

There Will Only Be Memories

As my aged eyes shed lonely tears. She tries so hard to be strong. Her little chin quivers, as she says, "It's all right Gran." She wipes my eyes. The victory of tears has won. Two twin tears run down her small face, as she gives a shaky sigh. Little does she know that through the coming years, as the excitement of teen-age years gets closer to womanhood, that through the coming years, there will only be memories of the one who cares so much. She'll go alone after I am gone. Maybe on certain days my spirit will walk beside her in the shadows, as her memories come alive when she remembers my teachings of yesteryears.

Throughout her life Gladys had a dream of ministering to her people in her own Ojibwa language. Her mother was a strong role model for this ministry. Her father was also a great teacher for her as she pursued her dream. She brought the gifts of spiritual teaching from her First Nation ways and from the sacred ways of the Christian community. Both these ways were a part of Gladys and could not be separated. That was her gift to us. She taught us to walk with respect and to honour the teachings from both traditions, seeing in both the profound teachings of God as Creator and Christ. She helped us to build bridges by sharing her full spiritual journey with us: her struggles in faith, her insights, and her teaching.

Learning Ministry from My Father

My father, James McCue, was always an elder looked up to and respected by the Indians of our reserve. Then as he grew older my brothers Austin and Leslie took over. They had learned all there was to know about the work he proudly performed for many years.

So many times way back when there was no road, no help would get to us, and when there was a need, my dad would go to do what he could to help the people who were sick. If there was a death he would conduct the wake, help shovel the snow at the home of the family. Then he would join up with the other men and they would trample the snow and shovel a road way up to the cemetery. Men and women helped every way they knew how. Sometimes if it was a man who died, and in those days times were pretty hard, someone would give their best coat and trousers so that the person would have a burial garment. It was always that way even when women and children passed away.

The wake was always a two-night ordeal. There was praying, singing and feasting, all night giving support to the bereaved even after the funeral. They were never cast off. People kept visiting, lightening the load of emptiness death leaves behind. Men would cut them wood. Women and children would carry it in or pile it near the kitchen door. Then they would share food with them for a long time. It seemed that people were so close to everyone in them days. It was such a good way. It was a good feeling of belonging, where you were a necessary person. Even if you didn't have book learning or a diploma, it didn't matter. It was love and pity for each other. That comes from God. The understanding love that knows no bounds that count. There was joy and satisfaction knowing you were doing your best, proving the love of our Creator and doing the work He expects us to do.

I wanted to follow in my father's footsteps, 'cause he seemed to be so happy helping people. A good life I thought. I will help my people, physically and spiritually. But this was God's work and I didn't know who he was. I would have asked him for help and support. I didn't know where to start. I knew that I couldn't do it alone. I kept putting it aside as I was bearing a family. All the while, all the time God had it all planned out. I started getting thoughts about my life.

I knew I was a weekend drunk but that was the only break I had after a week of hard work looking after the children, bent over the washtub, always the last one to eat. Sometimes there wasn't enough food. I saw more dinner times than dinners, so I looked forward to the weekends when I could forget. Then I noticed my children were drifting away from me. They had so little respect for me that it hurt. And in my foolish way I thought I was such a good mother, I didn't deserve that. So I decided to quit boozing around. I'd show them. Only to learn how much my children loved me. They supported me by their little kind acts and kisses. When I would feel let down, I'd cry for the want of drink, they would get me a towel so I could hide my tears. Oh my poor children they had so much patience with me, when my nerves were raw and I'd get cross, they would go and play in the woods until I called them home. It was as if nothing had happened. Gradually I got strong.

But tragedy was around the corner. Just when I was getting strong my baby got sick. She was so small and I loved her so much. When the doctor told me, "I can't do anything more. Take her home to die," I knew I lost what little faith I had in God because how could he take away my innocent baby who hadn't lived very long. This was like a knife in my heart. Once more I didn't know which way to go, turning back to the bottle seemed the only way out. But way down deep I knew that I would lose my children again. So the day I brought little Brenda Jean home from the hospital, I was once more a torn and tortured woman.

But again, my eyes tried to seek out God's face. In desperation I asked my daughter for a Bible. I knew there was never one in the house but she always went to Sunday school. She ran into the bedroom and came out carrying a small Bible wrapped in a cloth and said, "Here, mom." I took it, opened it. But there was nothing written in it, only red marks across the pages. I yelled, likely swore and threw the book on the floor. I walked into the bedroom. I looked at my baby sleeping so peacefully. I fell on my knees beside the bed and shouted, "Why God? Why are you doing this to me?" Then just like flipping the pages of a horror picture book, my life flashed by. Then I felt a heat so intense in my face, it was taking my breath away. I got so scared, I begged God to help me for I was dying. I don't know how long I pleaded, until I felt like I didn't have any clothes on. And the soft cool rain was falling on my body and the heat of sin was gone. I felt a hand on my head. I thought maybe my man came home. I reached up to where I felt the hand. There was no one there. But the feeling of the hand was still there. I opened my eyes. There was no one there, only my children who were crying. They were scared. But I felt so peaceful, My baby was awake. Her little arms held up with a smile on her face. Then I saw many faces of God through her eyes. I prayed once again. "And God, when the time comes, when she goes home, give me the strength and the faith to understand and learn me to depend on you, so I will get ready to meet you and my baby."

The children went out and got the Bible as it had fallen open. It was the 14th chapter of John: the promise of God's great love, a hope for a life when we go through this life on earth. On the 6th day of December exactly six months from the time she was born, even to the hour, she took flight to join our Creator.

I took the lining out of a coat—a gold-coloured satin—and made a burial gown for my baby. The best that I could make. But I know that God in his great pity for his children must have given her a white sparkle dress, and through her I found God, forgiveness and strength to live one day at a time, until the day when my spirit rises to greet the Creator. But until then I must work to be kind, pray for guidance, to weigh my feelings and do what is right, read to my people and guide them to heaven's shore. I must ask each morning what he wants of me and believe, as I lean on him, I will get strength to do my part. This is the life of an Indian elder. As servant of God ready to help not put myself above anyone, walk in humbleness, seeking always seeking his favour.

HONOURING THE ROOTS

When I first applied for a permit to work for my people, I was told that I'd have to go learn how to preach about our Creator's love for his children. So I decided to go to school. Then I was told I was too old and wouldn't qualify. I felt bad. But I didn't give up. I knew that I was going to work for a powerful God and nothing was impossible for him.

So, in 1980 I got a letter from Native Ministry saying I was picked to go to White Bear Reserve in Saskatchewan. I wanted so much to be a part of this but I didn't want to travel, leave my children. People said, "They are all grown up now. You stayed around them all the time. It's your turn to make something of your life." But no one knows a mother's heart, only a mother. I feared the unknown.

I even prayed about this. I'd work for the Creator but only in Curve Lake. God must have smiled, cause I talked to him person to person. But the more I backed away, the closer I felt to him. I got a phone call about two days before I was going, when I was thinking that God answered my prayer, and sent someone else. The call came saying, "You get the limousine from Peterborough. Your plane ticket will be at Terminal 2." So I packed my things and went.

I was so afraid to go by plane. Then I remembered what I said to my mom when I was going to England. She was so afraid for me. I said, "Mom, you're not to worry. God brought me safely to this world when I was born and he will take care of me all through this life until He comes after me." She said, "Thanks my little one, I only wanted to hear you say this. You know I've always trusted him, too."

So here again many years after the same words gave me courage. We got to Saskatchewan. It was summer camp: no running water, bunk beds, no bed clothes. We had to take sleeping bags. But it wasn't all that bad. I was no stranger to a little wash basin where I had to take all my baths besides do my washing in it.

A couple of days we went on a bus tour to Banff. So as I was nearing my destination, I looked up into the powerful mountains, God's wonderful creation, still I wondered why I had to go so far away. We stopped in one part, where two mountains were on opposite sides of our tour bus. We stopped and got out to get a better view. That is where I got my answer, that is where God spoke to me.

As I looked up into the trees passed up farther to the great boulders, that were so strong and so big, then to the snow capped mountains, it was like I was one of the smallest beetles of this creation, who lives there. Then like a friend beside me God put these words into my mind: "You're small compared to what you see, and you are feeling helpless, looking at the creation that seems too vast. As small as you are, I have a place for you in my work. Feed my sheep. Bring the word to my children. I gave you a language, enough understanding to read your Ojibwa Bible. Go be my messenger. I will give you what to say, when you are asked to bring a message." Then I understood. I didn't care who saw me. I just cried out and thanked my Creator in front of everyone there.

That is where I decided I would work for God by putting my life in his hands. I would get directions. He has taken care of me through my life. It hasn't always been calm waters for my fragile canoe. But he gives me strength to ride the rough waves. My paddle bends sometimes, the current is so strong.

But some day I will reach the Bay of Golden Peace. Maybe my eyes will be sightless, but with his love as my compass, I will hear him say in soft Ojibwa, as my birch bark canoe touches the shore and I feel his hand on my head, as I did the time I found him, when I was lost in the darkness and I was blind and couldn't see: "You've come home my child. Rest in my presence. I am still looking after you."

MEEQUACH: REFLECTIONS FROM THE FORT QU'APPELLE CONSULTATION

As a nation we must try to solve the more important parts and by sitting together, comparing our ideas, with the help of our Creator, the light will start seeping though this dark shadow that is so often the wall that we must overcome. Our people are getting educated. We are a strong people and it makes my heart warm. I can visualize Indian leadership like a searchlight beam showing across the cloudy sky from the four corners of this land, directing our younger generation to take up the work we are striving for. There's provisions for education, good resource centres and there are wonderful leaders.

FROM A NATIVE BAPTISMAL AT CURVE LAKE MINISTRY

We sit in a circle as we have always done in any important come together, for the circle signifies the circle of life. From birth until we complete the circle at death the circle of our environment, also the circle of our drum, reminds us all of the heart beat of every Indian Nation. The four corners of this creation where we are is held up by the four elders, who have their own purpose.

The elder of the North offers the gift of snow and cold air that causes everything to stop their motion, to rest for a season until the elder from the South offers the gifts of warm rain and gentle winds, awakening all that sleep, the trees and herbs, flowers and food.

Then the elder from the East, who is the Keeper of the Light, known to us as the Sun, offers the gift of light and illumination.

Then the elder from the West receives the Sun, who has completed the circle of another day. The other lights, the Moon and the Stars take their place in the sky, telling us of the changing of the seasons and the guiding of our direction. This is the work of the Creator.

Let us always be mindful of this love for us and thank him for who we are. We profess we work for him. Let us try our best to be good leaders and always ask him for directions before we start. For without asking for his help, who are we working for? Will each one who makes up this circle promise the Creator that you will help this child and direct its way to respect all creation and honour the ways of those who have gone before us. So with this eagle feather, we seal our vows, because the feather comes from the messenger who goes closest to the Creator, hearing our prayers from the beginning to the end of our circle. *Meequach.*

GOOD FRIDAY REFLECTIONS

I always feel sad on Good Friday. I would just like to go down to the woods, sit beside the tall trees and hear the breeze as it whispers hope to all the things that grow there.

NATIVE MINISTRY

Native ministry is a must. For when the roots of Indian culture die part of our religion dies, so does part of our people.

CIRCLE

When we come into a circle, we feel something good is about to happen. First we ask God to be in the centre and we draw from this warmth of the true meaning of Christian fellowship.

YAHWEH

In the ancient Hebrew texts, there were two words for "God." One was *Elohim*, which was a plural form. The other was *Yahweh* (in Latin *Jehovah*). The original Hebrew word *Yahweh* was written without vowels because in the times before Christ Hebrew language had no vowels. Therefore the original word for "God" was not *Yahweh* but *YHWH*. In ancient Hebrew *YHY* was the past tense of the verb "to be," while *HWH* was the future tense of this verb. Therefore *YHWH* expresses both the past and future of the verb "to be." In God we think of *YHWH* more as a noun meaning "being" and that's how we get the idea of supreme being or Creator that we call Lord or God. It is interesting that in Ojibwa *Wey-yah* means "someone," that is, a being. *Wey-yah* is merely a reversal of the two consonants *Yah-wey*, the later Hebrew word for a being.

PRAYER

Help me to remember no matter what happens, "Thy will be done." Dear Jesus, I cry for my *daunis*, my *kwus kee win* is so big it made me remember. You must feel this way when I'm bent with my heavy load. But I know that I am your child. Help me to live and respect all things. And walk with you in faith.

OF ALL THE WONDERS OF THE WORLD

Of all the wonders of the world no one seems to have ever tried so hard to find out why they were made or what they represent, as they do when they come across Indian artifacts.

Everything is done to find out why and what things meant. We are a people who like sharing our ways and knowledge about survival, how to manage in rough times. We are a people who find it a privilege to help any race.

We are a sharing people, even though we were considered pagan. We were all made out to be ignorant and wouldn't know when we were used or cheated. But no matter what race it is we know. There are aggressive races. Then there are meek races. Then there is always the third who dominate and believe there is no other way but their way. This is where the stem or the beginning of discord takes root. But all along the way the meek has been quiet about everything but learning as the years go. They learn how the game is played.

As I Sit Here

As I sit here alone in my house, I gaze out at the rain and I hear the mighty voice of the thunder and see the quick flash of lightning, just like the sharp knife trying to slice the clouds, so the sun can shine through again. The clouds felt the sharp stabs for they look ragged, like my oldest shawl; the thunder is kind. The sun will shine again tomorrow. The ground needed the rain. The grass and the trees were thirsty. Our invisible Friend. Her name is Nature. She knows so much. She is kind to us. She has washed the parched leaves that are faded. She will send the wind to guide them to their winter quarters.

Sacred Gathering

Once again I've returned to the sacred gathering place of my people. This is where they came to meditate and converse with their *manido*, to ask for directions and added wisdom to look into the future. Each one of the stumbling blocks that are discovered, here as we well as other places, gives warnings and tells of the things that have come to pass. Others which will happen, when the Native will be accepted and known that our ways and our beliefs are learned from nature, through the Great Spirit. When we lack wisdom we get it from looking at creation, that was made for us to learn from the animals, the birds, the inhabitants in the water. This is when I learn about medicine. Those we are looking for tonight tell us about the sicknesses that plague our nations today. It is written here, even though they were written many many years ago, even so long that the lichen has covered them. Like the cover of the Sacred Book, they still hold back the mysteries of the cure and the law of the curses that overpower the individual who refuses to respect the whole contents of this world—the trees, the grasses, and the roots. They all have the their own power to cure, but one must be able to recognize what you are looking for, for certain ailments.

Ears of Stone

I have come to the place of meditation
Of my ancestors.
I have visited in the moon
Of the falling leaves.
How still: how peaceful it is
This is hallowed ground.
(The birds. The trees.)
The murmur of the underground stream
Tells me I am standing
Where my people once came for knowledge
And to converse with the Gods.
I feel eyes are upon me.
I feel the breath
Of a dying breeze
As it passes,
Leaving the trees
to whisper a mystery
To me.
I have tried
I have tried
So hard to understand
But my ears cannot
Grasp the meaning.
But I must remember.
Oh ears of stone,

You are sharp,
Your mouth too is open,
But beyond your lips
Lie the unknown secrets
You hold.
Ah, you are too wise for me.
But I shall always be glad
That I am one, as of You.
Centuries ago,
You put your thoughts
On stone that would be seen
By people of all nations.
Only you
Hold the mystery
Of my people
white rock.

White Rock

I came to you rock of wisdom;
Reveal to me the meaning of my being.
Make me a wise and brave leader,
Or show me a way to cure our sickness.
And may I
Even as I grow weak from hunger,
Be ready to give thanks
For the water that whispers.
Be patient—
Send me my vision oh rock:
Release me from this temptation.
Take my spirit to the unknown world of wisdom;
So, as I return, I can prove
I am a true son
With a heritage of being brave

Steady and unmoving as you are
Unchanging with the moving of time.
Thank you white rock
For letting me be what I am—an Indian

Anishnawbe Signs

The swinging of my *bayou* as my baby sleeps (ahh!). If I could only go back, retrace my footsteps to these times. The smoke from the wood stove drifts lazily down. It bounces on the new fallen snow. This is a sign of a break in the weather. It's going to be mild, (*kah-gat*). The weather man said rain, too, but through the signs of our Nishnawbe ways we can always know the evening star lay in her bed of water last night. Soon it will rain *ke-sking-wam*.

Stories were important ways for the Ojibwa people to share teachings with humour and with dignity. We all learned to listen carefully for the stories as they were told and retold. Gladys had a special way of telling and re-telling stories:

Old Woman—*Knoj Qua*

We were camping on the shore of Spirit Lake. The men have been piling wood all day, so we can keep the fire going all night. Oh, it is so cold. There's no breeze. Soon the full moon will come out. There is tension everywhere. It is too quiet. Only the frost makes a shattering noise as it hits the trees. There is no animal or night bird's call. We are waiting for something to happen, but we don't know what. I am almost afraid to breathe. The hunger growl of our stomachs sounds like thunder, as we glance at each other. We drink some more cedar tea and take our *quop kes keen* and offer it around. It is comfortable in camp. But our minds and our spirits are restless. We don't know what it is. The feeling is with every one restless with fear. I look towards Knoj Qua.

Knoj Qua is getting on in years, but [is] very wise. She don't seem to be any different tonight. She gazes into the coals as she pokes the logs so they will catch fire. She turns her head sharply as if she heard something. Her eyes wander from one face to another as she pulls her shawl up around her head and makes her way outside. I hold my breath. She turns as she gets to the opening. There are tears in her eyes. She is crying softly. We all jump up and follow. She is nowhere. There is something way down by the lake. We all are afraid to go but Maung Zaus runs faster than anyone. He gets there first. He holds his hand up for silence. Knoj Qua is kneeling in the snow, her face turned toward the night sky.

There's northern lights in a circle right above our camp. They're in dancing motion all around. Only inside the circle it is dark. But there is a small white cloud in there. It looks like it is growing. We gaze forgetting about the cold. Slowly it takes on a form of a child. It is wrapped in white fur, which shows off its little brown face and black eyes. Look it is wearing a mist around its head and on the right side is a beautiful star. It makes rays toward the earth. It looks like a dew drop or frost on the trees, changing colours, like when the sun shines on the frost, the Creator is showing us; when the moon is at its fullest, it gives life to the earth. This little baby is a good sign. I can feel my heart. We have seen what we were waiting for. The Creator has given us a good sign. Let us sing. This happened a long long time ago, but each year when the time draws nigh again, we get that good feeling. That little holy Baby from the land of the northern lights is with us again

Gladys ended this story with a grandmother's prayer for her children.

Grandmother's Prayer for Her Children

The Creator forms each little child
long before its birth.
He watches over it and loves
it, until the time comes
when it leaves Mother's
body. The she in turn shares with others the
magic of the Creator's
gift. This has been
the meaning of Christmas from that
first day, when it was
shared with Angels

from on high. Now as we
offer gifts on this day. May
they be great or small. Accept
each one with thankfulness
for they are given with love.
Be warm. Gran.

Trees Full of Diamonds

The trees were full of diamonds this morning and the lake was beautiful. Before sunup the Windigoes must have had their council or maybe they were cleaning up. There are times I can't see the island. They can't be smoking the peace pipe. The smoke is too intense. The trees look so heavy with jewels. No king or queen saw so many as I've seen this morning. It is good to be able to see. I thank God.

Smoke Signals Across the Lake

I see the smoke of three camp fires
On this sunny March morning.
They come from the fires, built on the shore
By the Windigoes of the four corners
They meet here once a year to decide
The ways of the livelihood of their Nations
To smoke the pipe of peace.
They must have come to a good understanding
Because I see the sign of one single smoke
Where they have each put bits of tobacco.
That says there will be peace and understanding
With our Indian Nations.
So let us lift up our arms to embrace
The warm sunshine of our Mother Earth's love.
Let us feel the pulse of Nature's heart beat.
We will have the good feeling of
Belonging to our land, and to live
Keep it that way.

Don't Look at Me As a Nation

Don't look at me as a nation. I am an individual. I like to be a friend to everyone I meet. There's good and bad in my people as it is in other nations of this world. What I'd like is to be on equal terms, not only when I can help you, then you can set me on your back shelf of your closet memories until the next time you need me again. But I can't advertise for a friend. My friendship is 365 days and nights, 7 days a week.

Nii Gichi Noos: A Prayer

My refuge in my stormy life. No one else understands or cares what happens. It is not only that I am getting old. It is not the change that comes with age. My mind is still good. My body strong. My eyes still see the miracles of another new born day, another sunset with the colours of your creation of human people.

As time moved closer to her journey to the spirit world, Gladys reflected more and more on her life and what she had come to share. She often wondered whether she had taught us much. We do not wonder. We know what she has shared with us and we are thankful.

Like the Four Seasons

In the springtime of our lives there is so much to see, to experience; the joys and sorrows. They seem so brief, short lived because tomorrow will bring new ideas, new friends, a new outlook on life. It is so good to believe without worry, without cares, without responsibilities. This will change. It is too good to last.

In the summer of my life, I have conquered the first hell. Funny it used to look so big. Almost like a mountain, as I look around, I see the outlook of life. There is promises in every river, tree, lake, and the meadow is full of all kind of life. Her arms are loaded with flowers. The animals speak to me. I understand them. Even the trees wave their arms to me. They offer me rest. But I must keep going. There is so much to see and do. Oh it's so good to be alive. But the summer is short. All too soon I must start my way down. Funny it's not as hard going down as coming up. But I was younger then. But it's still good to be alive.

In the fall season of my life, the sun isn't as warm as it used to be or maybe my bones are thicker. It doesn't seem to warm me inside as it used to. I guess I will sit at home. I will watch the world from inside of my eyes, even when those aren't as keen and quick as they used to be. But, life has been good to me. I have no regrets.

The winter of my life is like the snow, that piles up and blows across the road, not making a straight line but a zigzag pattern. Those are my steps. The trees are dead looking, bare, rough bark, hanging loose, like my skin. The wind blows and shakes the faded grass like the wisps of my hair that won't stay in place anymore. But, however, it's been a good life.

When I stand among the shadows, in the twilight of my life. My sun is setting. I have gained my rest.

Gladys died September 11, 1993, after a brief illness. Although hospitalized when she was diagnosed with cancer, she insisted on going home to die. There, her family came to care for her and friends and relatives came to visit and pay their respects in the last few weeks before her death. She often asked to sit up in her chair, looking out over Buckhorn Lake and into the many colours of the sunset.

Glossary

bizindan weweni — listen carefully
Shognoshqua — white woman
meequach — thank you
daunis — my daughter
kwus kee win — afraid of or expecting harm from somewhere
manido — spirit or god
kah-gat — really, really
Nishnawbe / Anishnawbe — (both spellings are used) one who was lowered from the Creator
bayou — hammock, made for a baby, out of rope and a blanket
ke-sking-wam — pissed the bed
knoj qua — good woman
quop kes keen — bannock made on top of a wood stove
windigo — spirit being (may also be spelled *weedigo*)
Nii Gichi Noos — my grandfather (often used in prayer)

Photo by Alisa Clark

Gladys Taylor Cook

Recorded and edited by Joyce Carlson

Gladys Taylor Cook was born in August of 1929 in a tent, surrounded by fields of ripening grain at Sioux Valley First Nation, in western Manitoba. The first child of Ruth Wasuda Ross and Elijah Taylor, Gladys was brought into the world by a midwife, a grandmother from her community, with her father helping.

She was given the Dakota name Topah-hde-win at a special naming ceremony by her father's family. This name, meaning 'four steps,' suggests also 'help in the four directions,' the number four representing the four directions of the sacred circle of life in Dakota tradition.

She was later baptized Gladys Evelyn Taylor at St. Luke's Anglican, a mission church in Sioux Valley. Her mother and father had been married in that same mission church in an arranged marriage. Elijah Taylor had been asked to marry Ruth when she returned from residential school at the age of 16. Ruth had lost her own mother when she was only 14:

It must have been hard for my mother and father, being in an arranged marriage, and both being young. What I remember when I was very young is that my mother and father were very hard working people. We had a farm. My mother and father both worked hard to earn a living.

My father farmed his own land, as well as a piece of land which belonged to my mother. This land was a little distance away from where we lived. My mother always had a big garden and lots of flowers all around the house. We had horses and I used to love riding horses, especially bareback.

In our community, when a person lost her mother, as my mother did, someone else [would] often take over, adopt a person. My mother's aunt became my granny. I spent time with her when I was very young, when my mother was out working doing housework for people around the reserve. Later, when I was in residential school, my mother would arrange for me to stay a couple of weeks with her father's mother at Oak Lake near Pipestone every summer. I loved this.

In Dakota tradition, family relationships are very important. Ruth had been adopted by the family of her mother's sister, the Pratts of Sioux Valley, strong leaders and chiefs for generations. Gladys' father, Elijah Taylor, was born in 1908. His father had died when he was three weeks old.

A People Adapting to Change

Hardship was not new to Dakota peoples. Gladys was born 67 years after the Dakota peoples had fled massacres in Minnesota and North and South Dakota. Dakota history has been marked by the need to respond to massive change.

Historically, the Dakota of the Siouan language group occupied lands in the northwest plains, extending from Lake Superior in the east, west of the Red River and Lake Winnipeg to the edge of the northern boreal forest and south to the Minnesota River in South Dakota and southern Minnesota. The Cree, Ojibwa, and Assiniboine had acquired firearms a generation before the Dakota. By the early nineteenth century, Cree and Assiniboine were pushed further west by settlement and a decline in game. At this time the Dakota moved to their more southern territories in the central plains of Minnesota, as well as North and South Dakota.

In the War of 1812, Dakota peoples fought together with the British against the American colonists who were expanding into their lands. They were given assurances by the British that their land rights would be respected. The subsequent treaty between the British and Americans, however, betrayed these promises. After the War of 1812, treaties forced upon them by the Americans provided for the admission of whites to the Dakota lands.

Between 1815 and 1862 the Dakota became skilled farmers while continuing to hunt where game was plentiful. They were especially skilled with horses, having used them extensively in their plains hunting culture. Their agricultural expansion was slow, but definite. As settlement around their lands increased, hunting lands by which they had supplemented their incomes were settled. Game was becoming increasingly scarce, and they were being forced into the confines of reserves. Finally, in the summer of 1862, the Dakota attempted to reclaim their lives and land in an uprising. They were crushed.

Men, women, and children were slaughtered by American soldiers. A thousand survivors fled north to Red River remembering the promises of the British, and carrying medals given their ancestors from the War of 1812. Red River, a small colony of a few thousand, felt bound to honour the promises, but while they accepted the Dakota, they offered little assistance.

The Dakota succeeded in making the adjustment to the Canadian west through extraordinary resourcefulness and diplomacy. Between 1862 and 1870 when Manitoba became a province, the Dakota made peace with the Cree and Ojibwa First Nations as well as the Métis peoples who were inhabiting the territories where they wished to settle. Canadian settlement reached to just beyond Portage la Prairie, Manitoba, by the early 1870s.

The Canadian government intended the Dakota peoples to settle on one reserve. They disagreed and proceeded to select their own lands in several locations. They formed a loose confederacy of seven council fires or extended family groups based on location. Oak River, now called Sioux Valley, the first reserve chosen, was well beyond the established settlement area at Portage la Prairie. Located in the Assiniboine River Valley where it is joined by the Oak River 40 kilometres west of Brandon, Manitoba, it was selected in spring of 1875. By mid-summer, the families were working hard on their gardens and building homes.

The varied skills of the Dakota were necessary to make the transition to Canada. Considered "alien Indians," the government treated them differently than other First Nations. They were allotted lands on the basis of 80 acres per family of five. Other First Nations received 160 or 640 acres per family. Lands set aside for them were also much smaller in area than those taken up by European immigrant homesteaders. Their early attempts at farming were very successful. However, measures by government to control their economic autonomy created enormous hardship.

Early Years on a Farm

On a summer's day, the sky is wide above the valley. Clouds puff and billow above greening fields. Horses and cattle graze along hillsides and in the valley. The farmhouse where Gladys' family lived during her childhood years was on a hillside overlooking the valley.

Saskatoons, wild plums, and chokecherries grow abundantly along hillsides, ravines, and riverbanks throughout the valley. These wild fruits are picked and preserved to supplement produce grown in the garden.

Clusters of lilacs grew alongside her mother's flower gardens. Her mother's vegetable garden was cleared from a tall stand of oak. Nearby is the old homestead of her mother's family, her grandmother and grandfather Pratt, with another large garden area and giant willow trees that Gladys loved to climb.

Between the two farms is a special area that the Pratt family use for the sacred ceremonies in memory of departed family members. The Dakota were known to be an independent tribe, with strong spiritual traditions. When they began farming in Minnesota, Dakota leaders had engaged missionaries to act as farm instructors, and they translated the Bible and religious books into the Dakota language. When a number of Dakota leaders were hanged after resisting the takeover of their lands, they went to the gallows singing a Christian hymn in the Dakota language.[1]

The people of Sioux Valley continued to maintain their own spiritual and cultural traditions while they were strongly influenced by church teachings. In her grandfather Matthew Pratt's time, the family became increasingly involved in the Anglican Church. Her grandmother played the organ all her life, a total of 75 years until she was in her late eighties; her uncle, the Rev. Donald Pratt, was ordained as a young man. He has continued to farm while serving the local church.

Going Away to School

The Anglican Mission had established a small day school on the reserve and some children attended that school. Elijah Taylor had attended the day school, although he missed as often as he was able. He was caught by the Indian Agent numerous times, and roughly returned. His mother felt the school taught values that went against traditional teachings. Other children had to attend residential schools that were even more destructive of cultural values. Ruth Wasuda Ross, Gladys' mother, had been required to attend residential school.

The weight of Canadian law was behind the removal of children to residential schools, but the fact that the schools were run by the church may have assisted the community somewhat to accept this intrusion into their homes and families.

The small Anglican mission church on a hillside overlooking the valley was the centre of the community and a common gathering place.

In summers in Sioux Valley, we often had pow-wows. This was a really special gathering in our culture, a time of meeting new friends and old friends. It was a time of catching up with family news and activities. We found out who was new in the family, and who may have got married. Often, we hadn't seen each other since the last pow-wow.

A pow-wow was one of the last things done for us before we had to go away. Then, on the last Sunday at home, we had the Christian way of worship. We had a service at the church, with lunch after the service. During the summers we went with the deaconess and women missionaries who came around in caravans. They were good and kind to us. I have a lot of respect for the women of God who came to us on our reserve.

I was four when I went away to residential school. I'll always remember—I didn't want to leave my mother. My grandmother made me a beautiful string of beads when I left. She tied them around my neck saying, "This is so you'll know you're loved. Always remember this, no matter how far away you are."

When they took us away, I looked back and saw my mother crying. When I got to residential school, they took off all our clothes, and then they cut our hair, and they cut the string of beads from my neck, the beads my grandmother gave me. I cried in my own language "No! No! Don't do that! That's from my granny." I scrambled to try to pick them up; I was crawling on the floor clutching them, trying to get as many as I could. "Put them in the garbage," the woman yelled, and she hit me on the hand with a ruler to make me let them go. I managed to keep one by hiding it in my mouth. I was afraid to lose the tie with my grandmother. I kept that bead for a very long time. I didn't tell my grandmother what had happened. To tell her what had happened would have hurt her, so I carried that pain.

I'll never forget the first time I was caught speaking my own language. We were playing tag, a whole group of us, laughing and running around outside. One of the children was "it," and I tagged her. Being "it," she was now a "monkey" until she tagged someone else. Then she would tag her to be whatever she wanted to call her, and so we were having our fun. When I called in my language "monkey! monkey!" to warn the other children, I didn't even see the teacher standing close by, partly hidden by the side of a building on the girls' side.

She asked me what I said, and I told her, laughing. But she grabbed hold of me, took me to the bathroom and told me to open my mouth and shoved a bar of soap in my mouth. It was that old-fashioned strong soap we used to have. It just made me gag. I felt so sick. I tried to brush my teeth again and again. It took so long to get the taste of that soap out of my mouth. Sometimes I can still taste it.

The building was a large stone building with a high board fence at the back and all the way around the sides. At the front there was a picket fence, but the back was our playground. They used to send us all outside. We walked around and around that yard. The boys' side had a skating rink in the winter and the boys used to skate there. The doors were locked, and when it was cold we used to huddle around the corners of the buildings where it wasn't so cold. The snow was always piled so high that it was up to the fence. We climbed and slid on the snow pile. To try to go outside the fence was out-of-bounds for us.

The hardest thing about being in residential school was that I missed my mother. Being away from home at such an early age, I remember sometimes just wanting to be close to her, wanting to put my head on her lap, and have her hand on my head. In a way, what happened was that we became good friends, and I've always been close to her, respected her, and learned from her. That special mother-child bond didn't change after I went away to school.

Our small family changed in another way, however. In the first year I was away, my mother and father parted. I found this very hard.

Both my parents were very strong people, coming from very strong families on the reserve. People have said they were very good people. They were hard workers, strong believers in the traditional culture, in a good way. I had to adjust to their parting.

My mother later formed a relationship with my stepfather and they had eight children, so she had a lot of responsibility. I'm sure she must have felt torn at times because of the two families, and me from the first marriage, and being the oldest. Yet, she always welcomed us home and tried to do special things with us. When I was very young, I know my mother did things with us. She gave us self-esteem. She did things to make us feel good about ourselves. This is deeply instilled in us. I've always had that little bit of memory, and I've always held on to it, all through my life.

She was a good cook. She could make a meal almost out of nothing. She would make a nice soup and add lots of vegetables. Sometimes after supper, she would help whoever was doing the dishes by putting them away. When the stove was cool enough from the cooking, we'd clean and polish it for the next day. She was fun loving, and we could always tell when she was hurrying us in this way, that we were going to have fun that evening. When the work was done, we'd run outside and play ball with her. She enjoyed playing baseball. These were some of our really fun times together. We'd wash those pots and pans really fast. She was a good hitter. When she got to third base, we'd always let her walk home.

She'd sing. Sometimes she'd ask "What did you learn in school?" It was her way of saying she was quite aware of what was going on in school. She was aware of the negative things because she and grandmother had attended residential school. My mother had attended school in Portage la Prairie. She never spoke of what she herself had gone through in residential school, but she gave us opportunity to talk about our experiences, whether they were good or not good.

I remember once talking to my mother about the baths we had at residential school. I remember saying when it was bath day, I really tried to be first in the tub. Three of us would bath together in one tub. The ones who were first had clean water. After that, everyone bathed in the dirty water. My mother was shocked. She said, "They have running water. Couldn't they let you bath in clean water?" She understood why I'd want to be first. It made me understand that she really knew what we were going through.

It was hard to get used to their ways of doing things, and it was always so lonely. When we went to bed at night, we missed our homes. I did a lot of crying. I was lonely, afraid, and living in fear. We were also hungry. We never seemed to have enough to eat.

One of the bad things was that we learned to lie and steal. We had to, to protect ourselves. It really bothered me because I knew that this was wrong. This was something I could never do at home. I would never do this to my own mother. We were taught to treat each other with kindness, honesty, and respect. It was hard that all of the treatment we received was in the name of God, because they were church people.

Christmas brought a break in the monotony. We had a nice turkey and plum pudding dinner at Christmas. Sometimes I think about those plum puddings. I loved those plum puddings. I never had anything like it again, the pudding was so good, with the sauce on it.

I used to make beautiful cards and send them to my mom. She always saved them, and when we came home in the summer, she'd bring them out and show us what we'd sent, and talk about how she felt about the card. She'd talk about what a nice picture it was. Sometimes, she'd come out to see us at Christmas, she'd come to the concert.

Gladys attended residential school for 12 years, until she was 16. At Elkhorn, children studied half days, and worked half days. After 12 years, Gladys received a grade 8 certificate as well as a bronze medallion for being a "good all round" student. While only 75 kilometres from her home in Sioux Valley, attendance at the school isolated her from family and community. She visited her family only in the summers for six weeks.

Gladys' mother attempted always to turn to see the positive side, and encouraged Gladys to do the same, although her own family also had resisted the idea of education and residential school.

In our extended family, we were adopted by my mother's aunt, Granny Pratt, and called her *Kunsi*, 'Grandmother.' My mother's dad's family were from near Pipestone, at Oak Lake Reserve. Mother's dad was the grandfather I knew best, and I spent time with him in the summer. His mother, whose name was really Granny Jackson, was my great-grandmother. We called her *Kunsi*. To better identify which grandma we were talking about, we called her "old granny" because she was the older of our grannies, and sometimes we called her granny Pipestone because she lived near Pipestone, a distance away from us. She was a very staunch native person. She didn't speak English. I remember her asking, "Why school?" and she was told, "We had no choice." It was explained that we were being taught so that we would be able to get an education and go to work.

My stepdad just laughed at that. He said, "That doesn't fit in, who is going to hire you? We will never be hired! Nobody will hire us! It's all for nothing." I remember him saying that. My mother felt differently. She encouraged us in her quiet way. She encouraged us to try to learn. She said, "It's going to help you make something of yourselves."

An important learning from my mother was to turn things around into the positive. If one can be positive, we can turn things around into a different perspective. I remember at home, my mother invited people to come over. We would prepare food and put on a clean dress. If they didn't come, my mother was very casual. She'd say, "Well, something must have happened. They must have had something else to do." She'd say, "Be positive. Look at things in a different perspective. Hope everything will be all right."

Another person who was really positive was a teacher whose name was Mrs. Hamilton. After I left school, I'd call her Granny Anne. She helped me to love learning. I loved poetry, and reading. I used to want to read all the time. I'm sure sometimes I was reading when I should have been doing all sorts of other things, like housework. Granny Anne was the person at the school who helped me with my studies, who showed me the most love. I think that at the school she was the person who helped me to understand what the love of God might really be like.

As children, we found some special things to do that brought happiness. We used to feed the chickadees on the window sills. I don't remember who started this, but we all tried to keep it up over all the years we were there. We put out little bits of bread crumbs, then we watched the birds when they came. They were so pretty to see.

In school, Gladys recalls the children at times had a lot of fun among themselves. They learned to sing and to play games such as ball. Their school competed against others at field days. This competition was sometimes difficult for children. Some of her cousins were in schools of different denominations, in Brandon and Saskatchewan, and they competed against each other, at times with some animosity. However, Gladys learned to play ball very well. Her mother's positive attitude helped ease some of her loneliness. "Don't do anything to make yourself feel bad," her mother said to her.

Early Trauma

As a very young child, Gladys enjoyed learning, and was a bouncy, outgoing, and exuberant child. Then, one year when she was around nine years old, her mother and stepfather noticed a change in her. She was no longer the bright-eyed, laughing, and bouncy little girl she had been. She was fearful and afraid. When they asked what had happened, Gladys explained:

We slept in large dormitories, all of us together. One day, I was in bed, alone, in the middle of the morning. I was nine years old. I had the mumps, was feeling really sick and sleepy. I remember the sides of my face were really puffy and swollen. A man, a staff, came into the room and to the side of my bed. He pulled the covers away. I pulled them back. He pulled them away and I pulled them back up again. I tried to slide down under the covers, I was so afraid. I cried out. He told me "Shut up!" And he hit me on the mumps side of the head so hard, I just felt terrible flashes of pains all up the side of my head. I cried and cried and put my hands up to the side of my head. The pain kept shooting and shooting through my head, and I found out later that my eardrum had been ruptured. He had hit me on the side of my face which was swollen with mumps with such force that blood came from my ear. I couldn't protect myself, and my head hurt so much, I couldn't keep him away. And he was a big man. Before he left, he threatened me. He said, if I told anyone, "you'll get it again." Then he left.

I was all alone. I tried to get up. There was blood running down my legs and on my hands and the side of my head. I didn't know what to do, or where to go. I crumpled on the floor in my nightie. Another girl found me there, and thought I must have cut my hand, because there was blood all over my hand. She called the nurse. The nurse must have known I'd been raped. She took a sheet and wrapped it around me, washed me, and took me to the doctor's house in Elkhorn. Days later, when I returned to school, the kids asked "Is your hand okay?" I said it was, but I wondered why they asked about my hand. I thought later that they probably told the kids I'd hurt my hand.

This was the terrible thing. There was no one to protect us. When the nurse took me to the doctor's house at Elkhorn, they must have known. The nurse must have known when she wiped the blood from my legs before she took me. All things were kept quiet. No one ever asked me what had happened, and I never said anything to them. It was only my mother that I talked to.

I suffered permanent damage to my eardrum as a result of the blow. I felt very guilty, as though it was my fault. I was so young, and I wondered what I had done. At times, I really blamed myself. I wondered what I had done wrong. I thought, "If only I hadn't been sick!" After that I tried to stop myself from being sick. If I hadn't been alone, maybe this wouldn't have happened.

We really tried to watch out for each other. We had to. When I was older, as part of our jobs, we were asked to work in the homes of staff members, doing housework or babysitting. We knew that we might be attacked, but we had to go. If we said no, we would be punished for talking back. Once, I remember being asked to babysit for this same man. I was so afraid, but I was afraid of being punished, of what they would do if I didn't go. The house was outside the fence and the compound where the school was, and after I looked after the children, he was walking me back to the residence when he raped me again. It was dark, and late, and there was no one around. It happened two more times after that. This was why we were terrified of being alone, of working outside the residence in the homes of the workers. But, it was hard because we were assigned jobs, and these were our jobs.

I remember one of the girls was sent by staff to work and she refused. She didn't want to go, and so she fought. She fainted. I sometimes think, "At least she fought, she didn't have to go." We all knew that there were certain times that we were in danger. I was afraid to say no, somehow. I was afraid of being whipped or punished. And it was not all the time that it happened. It's just that we never knew when it might happen, and so we were afraid all the time.

I talked to my mother about this. I told her what had happened. Some of the other girls couldn't talk about what had happened to them when they were abused. We were all afraid.

> Gladys was raped when she was very young, and again when she was 13, 14, and 15. In her final term in school, together with some of the other young women who were similarly assaulted, Gladys informed the principal, describing what had happened. He promised to investigate. Gladys found out later that he, in fact, did not act on their complaint.

My mother went to the principal and talked to him. He said, "I'll look into this." By this, my mother felt that he would take care of what had happened. She trusted him because he was a man of God. My mother went to his office and he had her sign a paper he had prepared. I was sent to the office to fetch something and what caught my eye was the word "false" on a paper. I discovered the paper that she had signed on his desk. He had them sign a paper saying that what we said was false! I lashed out. I said, "That's not false! You can do anything you want to me, beat me up, strap me, but don't hurt my mother like this." I was sent to bed without supper for punishment.

My mother didn't tell my brothers and sisters what had happened. She did this to protect me. She never said anything, but she treated me with special care. I feel she must have talked to Grandma Pratt, because she often talked to her about things. I know she talked to grandfather about it. Years later, my stepfather told me "You'll never know...many's the night I held your mother while she cried and cried for you, knowing what it must have been like, helpless to do anything to protect you."

When I heard the Primate's apology [see Appendix One: Apologies to Native People], I felt my mother's presence. She had really trusted that when she talked to the principal, he would try to help the situation, he would put it right. She would never betray us and say it wasn't true. She would never have signed the paper if she knew what it said. After the apology, I felt that the wrong that had been done had at least been acknowledged.

Gladys found out years later that if the injury to her eardrum had been properly treated, she may have retained some hearing. Because the rupture went untreated, she has had to live with the hearing loss.

The healing of the emotional scars caused by the abuse has been a lifelong journey. At the time, Gladys was helped in dealing with the abuse by her mother's love and special care for her. Her mother considered Gladys' feelings and understood her turmoil. She also knew that her mother would never wish to cause her embarrassment and therefore would never talk to her brothers and sisters about the abuses, keeping it a private matter. Her mother's uncle gave Gladys the name Wakan-maniwin, meaning 'woman who walks with the Great Spirit.' Her mother's father, a healer in the Dakota tradition, also played a special role in helping her see herself in a positive way.

My grandfather gave me special quality time and teachings. I went to some ceremonies with him. He often worked with people who were sick, and he wanted me to be there. He would pray so that they would get better, or, if they were dying, that they would go on their journey. I used to go with him, and sometimes my mother went as well. My grandfather wanted me to sit with a man who was dying and hold his hand. The idea was to have purity from a young woman.

I questioned him when I was about 13 or 14 because I felt that perhaps I wasn't pure enough to help him in his work because of what had happened to me. He said, "You have been made a woman before your time," and perhaps because I seemed upset, he said, "You are pure in my eyes." He made it clear to me that it was all the more important for me to go to the ceremonies. I'm sure he was praying for me too because of what had happened to me.

Sometimes he'd walk by me, tap me on the shoulder or touch my head. His way of letting me know he cared and [he] loved me was to have me...with him. I sometimes used to hold the rattle. The rattle was used to call the spirits to come and help us because we need them. I used to get a little tired and go too slow, and he would tap me on the elbow or say, "Try harder *awijaka*," meaning 'hurry up' so I would speed it up.

I left school in October. It hurt me that they seemed to feel it was so important to go to school that they would take us from our families. By September I hadn't had any notice not to go back, and so I had actually started school. When they found out that I had reached my sixteenth birthday, they told me I had to go, even though it was into the school year. I had to give up my bed for someone else who was eligible for school.

Reflections on Cultural Differences

When Gladys left school, she had high hopes. She excelled at school, loved learning, and had her sights set on becoming a nurse. She was also a wonderful baseball player. After playing on the residential school team where her skills shone, she was invited to pitch on a semi-professional team. She practised a number of months, but was unable to continue into the season because she couldn't afford the team uniform. Baseball remains a great love.

After 12 years in school she believed she had attained a grade 8 education. Equivalency tests at the local high school revealed she had attained only a grade 4 to 6 level. She felt let down. While she could have managed working and going to high school, she couldn't see herself going back to sit with little children in grades 4 and 5. She couldn't afford to take night school to upgrade herself, and so she returned for a time to the Sioux Valley. She was in her late teens, and her family suggested the possibility of arranging a marriage. Gladys resisted, and feels in retrospect that her mother understood that marriage may have been difficult for her and respected her decision.

Gladys reflects on the learnings in school, on the contrast between those learnings and the understandings she had from her parents, and on her life after residential school.

Knowledge is a beautiful thing to have. It is the Creator who gave us the ability to learn. However, knowledge [education] is not the end in itself. Knowledge without wisdom or humility or love is like a person planning life without taking time to live. This is how I understand knowledge now, and a lot of our learning about living took place in the summer, in the care of our parents and grandparents, learning about life.

Sometimes I think we are always complaining about something. We say there is too much rain, or snow, or it is too hot or too cold. However we think about the weather, it stirs me to remember what my mother said: There are two things we can't do anything about, people and weather.

My grandfather in his wisdom and teachings shared a story once about this while visiting us at home. A storm was coming. You could hear thunder miles away. "Listen to that," he said, "hear that grumbling and rumbling away, and the flashes of lightning. It's kind of like the dispositions of people." I remember looking up at him, kind of not really understanding what he was saying. He continued, "When the thunder grumbles and cracks, it shows its temper. It's the grandfather telling us that's the way we sound, sometimes when we get carried away with ourselves. We have to constantly check out our behaviour because of the thunder and lightning within us." This teaching was a good lesson. "Why so many wars?" he asked. "Why so many people fighting against each other? Small groups of people hurt each other. We talk about harmony, but I don't know how we can understand if we don't talk about it, if we don't practise it. How can we understand what it means if we don't apply it? There's lots of things people don't have to work at, to be kind to each other and to smile every day."

My grandfather's words remind me of a poem I have learned about healing. We have to be careful with words, with the way we talk to each other. One word sometime can confuse a whole meaning, a whole expression. Our parents taught us by example. We had to work hard, but we learned a lot from working with them.

All of us children had duties in the summer. One of our chores was to keep five large barrels filled with water in the summer. My mother's big vegetable garden and flowers gave us a big job. We had to get water. One barrel had to be kept full all the time for household purposes and washing and for the garden and flowers and to wash our hair, and keep ourselves clean.

West of Brandon, in the valley, there were lots of berries and wild fruit. We picked them and made preserves. Our people were enterprising and hard working. Breaking the land, our people managed to grow good fields of grain. We took the grain on a wagon to a mill in Virden to have it ground into flour. We came home with bags of flour to sustain some of the families that had helped out. Sometimes we would exchange a load of wood for bags of flour. We wouldn't take anything without offering something in exchange. Today, so many think that we have always had handouts. There is so much stereotyping. People don't understand. We were judged and condemned before we had a chance.

When one lives with the people and sees how we lived, one understands we were hard working. We always had food on the table, and my mother worked in such a way that food went far. There wasn't always meat, but we always had vegetables. When my mother worked at a farm, she brought home milk. It was a combination of foods we had available.

What kind of an education were they giving us at residential school for our future? For our lives? I thank God for the common sense of my mother and grandmother, for their encouragement to think things out for myself, to make my own decisions. We made our own decisions, however right or wrong, and learned from them. We were self-taught, but we had the help of our elders, parents, and families if we needed them.

My family have been very involved in the Anglican Church. We had very dedicated lay readers and my uncle Donald had been ordained an Anglican priest. We had an Episcopal minister friend from Nebraska who came to stay in Sioux Valley every other summer. From the time I was young, I used to enjoy helping in the church, being up at the front during services. I loved reading, and I used to read a lot at home, too. I suppose it was natural that I felt comfortable reading and leading in prayer. The friend from Nebraska offered to have me come to do some work for him in Nebraska.

My mother encouraged me to go, saying, "You'll do all right!" She said they liked the way I felt comfortable up at the front.

New Opportunities

After staying a few months with the minister and his family in Nebraska, Gladys moved to Yankton, South Dakota, to work on housekeeping staff in a Roman Catholic hospital. She lived in the residence and became very close to the nuns. They invited her to become Catholic. She reflects on why she felt comfortable with them:

After being in residential school for so long, I understood the routine of an institution. The nuns were very good to me, and I felt comfortable in that structure. I really enjoyed the work. But, I was young and enjoyed life as well. I fell very much in love with a young man whose family lived in the area. He said that he loved me, and I believed him. In the past, the men had simply wanted sex and taken me.

I liked the attention from this man, and thought I would have a stable life with him. He said we would get married. I became pregnant and then the trouble began. He treated me really badly. The nuns were really disappointed in me, but they helped me as much as they could. When they had invited me to become Catholic, I just couldn't because I had been Anglican all my life. My belief was strong. Yet, I appreciated all they did for me.

The nuns helped me. They sent me to another Catholic hospital when it came time to have my baby girl. She was so pretty. She was born on St. Patrick's day. But one day, when I went down to the nursery to see her, she was gone! Her father's family had come and had taken her away. The hospital had somehow let them do that.

I sat down on the steps looking into that nursery and cried. I couldn't understand why they would do that to me because I was the mother. When I think about it now, I think I was so young, and so used to people simply doing things to me, and me just having to accept it. I didn't know what to do, except just sit down and cry my heart out.

His family took her and were looking after her. Then, one day, there was a fair; there were booths everywhere. All of a sudden, I saw one of his sisters coming through all the noise and the people and the booths holding my baby in her arms! I was so shocked! I could tell my baby was sick! She was tiny and you could just see she hadn't been looked after. The sister came up to me and said, "Here, if you want your baby back, you can have her!" I took her in my arms, and I rushed past all of those booths straight to the hospital with tears streaming down my face.

I saw her every day, and she was well-looked after. She started to turn rosy and pink again. Then, just as she was getting better, the family of the man came and took her again! I was so completely devastated. I kept trying to get her back over the next few months.

When she was about six months old, I met my future husband. He was from the same community, and he made it clear he would welcome my little girl into our home if I could get her back.

Gradually we just came to know each other, until finally he said, "So, when are we going to get married?" He gave me some money to buy my wedding ring. He gave me $20, I remember, and the ring cost about $13. My husband didn't wear a ring because of his work. That was a new beginning, and it looked good and made me feel happy.

My mother always said to look at the family of a person you are considering marrying. I did look carefully at my husband's family. They were solid, church-going people, and I've always got on well with them.

We were married in a small ceremony in Vermillion, South Dakota, east of Yankton. I remember I had a little pillbox hat, and a light pink eyelet dress. His business was doing very well. He co-owned a tree-trimming business. He was very busy doing contracts with hydro and telephone companies. He had trucks and equipment and worked out of town.

My husband was good in many ways. We lived next door to a person who was quite handicapped. On my way home from work, I would call her from the store, and I would buy her groceries for her, just as a favour. I never expected anything in return. But then there was a misunderstanding. She accused me of taking money. Two detectives came to my work place to question me. I had to go to the station after work, but before my work day was over, they came back and said she had found the money. I didn't go right home. I waited for my husband to tell him what had happened.

I felt really badly. They didn't trust me. They apologized, and realized they'd made a mistake, but we felt hurt. My husband said, "That's it! We'll move!" So we moved. Eventually, we had our own little house.

Our first child was a little girl we named Ruth after my mother and mother-in-law. She had a heart defect, and so died 17 days after she was born. Then our son came along.

I so enjoyed fixing up the house, sewing curtains, and making it nice. I've always liked to do housework, and to have my own house and make it nice was really fun. We had a garden and a fence. My husband looked after all the bills, and it seemed natural and right. He was used to looking after money, because of his business.

He was a drinking man, but I didn't realize how bad it was at first. I was still working at the hospital and as a cleaning lady for other people, although I was expecting our second child. There were times I asked for payment in groceries instead of in money. Other times, I'd pick up groceries on the way home to be sure we'd have food. My employer understood.

One day, a man from the store came to pick up my sewing machine. I felt so bad. I thought my husband had been keeping up the payments. I had so appreciated being able to have the machine to fix things up in the house. Then, the day came when I arrived home after a weekend visit to my mother-in-law and the house was boarded shut. I was so upset. I went running down to the person we were buying the house from. He lived on the corner near where the house was. He looked at me strangely. He was kind really, and he said, "You really don't know, do you?"

I cried and he held me. He told me the house payments were very far behind. My husband hadn't told me any of this. He'd had warnings, but he hadn't told me and so we lost everything. I didn't have a chance to get my personal belongings. If he had only told me, I would have had a chance to take at least my very personal things before the bailiff seized everything. He always said he was "looking after things." He didn't like me to question him. I said to the owner when I found it all boarded up, "Please just let me get my baby clothes and crib, and my photographs!" He said that he was sorry, but it was out of his hands. He couldn't do anything about it now.

Everything that I had ever owned was inside the house, and boarded up. My baby clothes, my photographs, my wedding dress, my medallion from residential school. The only thing to do was to go to my mother-in-law's house and live with her. By this time, our son was four and our daughter was 13 months.

I found out then that my husband had also lost the trucks and his business. His brother who was his hired man was also drinking, and so things got worse and worse. When they went out and I thought they were working, they were really drinking.

The spiritual things kept coming back when I was down. The Dakota church group that I was a part of brought things and somehow suddenly I had the basics I needed for the children. The church community had been part of my life from the time I first went to South Dakota. I began to go to the Episcopal church where my mother-in-law was involved. I am surprised when I think about it now, but I was very involved for one so young. I was just in my early twenties. There was a regular Episcopal church service with a priest in Yankton, but the Dakota people in the community organized church services in each other's homes. For a baptism, we went to the Episcopal church in town. But, much of the time, we had our own services, in our own language in our own homes and with our own families. These were memorable spiritual times.

We borrowed each other's homes if the houses were too small for the number of people. Even though my marriage seemed to be breaking down, this group kept me going. The people there called me Peacemaker. I think it was because I was from outside the community, so I didn't know people's relationships with each other before I got there. I was always trying to bring peace and harmony wherever I went. I encouraged people to get along with each other. I carried understandings of the church, and also understandings of my own culture, and found ways of putting these things together. I had the church structure in my life. It helped that we had translations into Dakota language.

During this time as well, I got to know a Native man who was with the Church Army in the Episcopal Church and so I went with him sometimes to help. He had invited me to join him. I actually thought about joining the Church Army and working with them as well, but when I talked with him about it, he seemed to have so many rules that he had to follow. While I was prepared to work with the people and help them to hold their own services in their own languages and with understanding of their own culture, I wasn't prepared to follow all those rules.

Our Dakota church group did really well. It was hard work, but together we accomplished a lot. We bought a portable organ so that we could carry it from home to home to have with all our services.

We used to think of all sorts of fundraising events. We'd plan about six months ahead for different events. I remember once we put on a little fair, with booths and we were selling handicrafts and baking that people had made. We had games to play, and we blew up balloons. It was like a carnival in the local church basement! We had a lot of fun sometimes. Once I dressed up as a gypsy. I borrowed my mother-in-law's dress, and wore big chunky earrings. I had a bracelets and necklaces, and I told pretend fortunes.

We made soup and sandwiches and cakes. We grew plants and then auctioned them. I was asked to do a lot of things. I found I could "act" out of a sense of humour. Being the youngest in the group, I found I sometimes felt shy, but underneath I wasn't. We were having fun while working. We made baby clothes and kitchen tea towels and pot holders and hooked rugs. The things we made got to be quite popular at sales. We sometimes had things that were brand new, especially close to the Christmas sales. That was all a good experience. While we had to have help for baptisms and funerals, we did everything else ourselves. When we raised funds, we collected in three pots. We had one collection for the support of the non-Native church and another for our Dakota people who were sick, for their medicines and food. A third was fundraising for special projects like purchase of our portable organ, or for hymn and prayer books in our own language.

I really got to know the women well, and enjoyed them. I was especially close to my mother-in-law and to my husband's sisters as well. I spent a lot of time in church activities. This sometimes made my husband mad. I remember once when he got drunk, he said, "Why don't you move to the church?" I left once, but my mother-in-law coaxed me to come back. She had had a stroke.

After we lost our house and moved into my mother-in-law's house, things got worse. There was beginning to be violence. It wasn't so bad when he was just hitting me. When he hit our son, I was really mad! I said, "You can do anything to me, but I'll be damned if you'll hit our son!" He flew into a rage. The next thing I knew, I woke up in the hospital. I had been beaten badly. Even then, I wasn't ready to leave my husband, but I knew that there was another way to live. I knew it would be possible to have a quiet home life, but I thought maybe it would get better if we could move into our own little place again. It was so crowded trying to live with the children in my mother-in-law's house. I had looked for a place, and I even found one I thought we could move to. I tried to tell my husband. I said, "I want to move...." What he didn't let me finish saying was, "into a place of our own." I was trying to say it in a nice way. He just screamed at me, "Well, get the hell out then!"

I was relieved when he said that. Suddenly, I knew I could leave. What he said helped me to know I was looking for that something better I had always known about. My mother-in-law tried to coax me to stay. But I didn't know if I could live in the area with him there close by, but not looking after me and the children. I felt I had done all I could. I felt at peace with my mother-in-law and with his sisters and the people of the church and community.

We had been together a total of seven years from the time we first met until the time I left.

I decided to go back to Canada. My mother-in-law took me to the bus. As I was leaving, just as I was on the steps of the bus—she took the ring off her finger. It was a beautiful gold band with one diamond. It was an expensive ring, and I knew it meant a lot to her. She loved me and didn't want me to go. We hugged each other, and I cried, and then we left, the children and I.

I left at 7:00 p.m. from Yankton, and arrived in Brandon, Manitoba, thirty-three hours later at 4:00 a.m. I had sent a telegram to my mother to let her know that I was coming home, but the telegram was put in their mailbox in the nearby town of Griswold. I arrived before she had received the telegram. She wasn't expecting me and the reserve was 40 kilometres from Brandon. I thought I would rest, clean up before we went to the reserve, but the hotel wouldn't give us a room. Then I went to the Y, and even the Y wouldn't give us a room! I sat on a bench outside the bus depot with my two children. They were hungry and tired. I asked myself, "What do I do now?"

I took a taxi all the way to Sioux Valley, arriving about five in the morning and woke up my family. I remember my mother just looked at me. My stepdad said after a while, "Something is not right."

They hadn't seen the children before, and they gave the children attention, making us welcome. My stepdad started making a fire to cook some food to feed the children. Suddenly, I noticed my mother was gone. I asked my stepdad, "Where's mom?"

He said, "She's gone to give thanks." She had quietly slipped outside. When I went out, I found her kneeling in the bush at the back of the house, and she was weeping as she was praying.

As she wept, she was saying things to make me think. I wanted to ask questions, but I knew better. I just knelt beside her. Now that I think about it, I wonder what she thought when she saw me. What a different person I was than the young woman so full of hope she had sent off a few years before. I had been happy and looking forward to life, to working. Now, I was skinny and haggard; I had sometimes gone without food to feed the children. My front teeth were missing.

I'll never forget those moments when we were together as she cried. I cried with her. There were no questions asked about the situation until I was ready to talk about it. My mother and everyone else respected this. I knew from the past, one just pays attention, and listens, and tries to figure out the meaning. One just can't ask questions, at least then.

For three weeks, I felt free. I had many good nights of sleep. I visited different people, introduced the kids to their relatives, and enjoyed being home. Then, it suddenly struck me. I had nothing. I had no marriage. I had no home. I had complete responsibility for the children, and I was all alone. What was I going to do with myself? I had no skills to work. The only thing that I could do was housework or work in a hospital.

I stayed with my family on the reserve for a while. My mother used to do housework and sometimes I'd go to help her in whatever way I could. When she washed clothes, I'd help her by hanging up the clothes.

I remember climbing up on a little platform, and pulling the clothes-line along, looking out as I was hanging the clothes. Later, I went out working on my own. My mother stayed home to bake bread or put her garden in, and I worked in her place. My mother was a good worker. I had to work really hard to keep up to her reputation.

After a year, the chief came and told me that I couldn't stay any longer with my mother and stepfather. I had married outside the band, and there was a rule that anyone who wasn't a band member couldn't stay on the reserve more than a year! The chief said to stay with my mother's friend who was living on a farm just off the reserve. After a few days I could come back.

About six months later, I found a job at the residential school in Portage la Prairie. My parents encouraged me to take it, and offered to look after the children for me.

I found working in the residential school to be all right. I worked in the laundry and sometimes at supervising the girls. Because of my own experience, I was able to look out for the girls as much as I could. There was a man on staff who used to come around when the girls were in the showers. He would go into the change rooms and locker rooms without knocking. It frightened them, and so we had a system. One of the girls would get up on a stool and look out the window when the girls were in the showers. When she saw him coming, she'd yell at me. I was always in the laundry near the showers, and I'd run and tell the girls. They'd scramble out of the shower so that whenever he came, he'd find nobody was there. I found this difficult, but tried my best to help them, and the job was good for me, with steady pay.

My mother worked at times for a teacher, and I could phone her there to check on the children. They told me if the children needed anything, and I would send money home. It was good for the children to be with my father and mother who taught them traditional ways. They were taught well. My parents were strong people who had come through a lot. My children were taught nothing is impossible if the Great Spirit is included in life, and not to take advantage of what is good. They were taught to meet people halfway, and to learn to give and receive in a good way.

I found it hard being so far away from the children. Every time

I went home, it was harder. After about a year, I decided to have them move closer to me. I was living in the residential school at Portage la Prairie, and I arranged for foster care for them until I could find a place for us to rent when we could be together. When I was working at the residential school, all the staff were requested to live in. I left the residential school, and began working at the hospital because I wanted a place to live with my children.

It was really hard to find a place to rent in those days. People didn't want to rent to a Native person. Finally, I found a basement apartment that we could move into. It was really small, but at least we could be together, and was really close to a good school they could go to.

After that, we rented a small house where we could stay. It was the first real home I'd ever had, and it was there that I really raised the children. I did try to find a larger house, but I was told the neighbours wouldn't want an Indian family close by. Our house wasn't a fancy house, but I fixed it up nicely. I was in new surroundings, with new activities, and meeting new friends. It was a fun time and I forgot a lot of the sadness.

When the children were young, there were times when I was really lonely, and did things I really wasn't proud of later. It was my first experience of freedom and going out and being with other people, meeting friends was really exciting. I began to get into drinking, but deep down I always knew there was a better way of living.

From time to time, I read teacups for people. Perhaps it was part of the wisdom I was taught that helped me to know a bit about human character. Whatever it was, people used to come to me from time to time and they found it helpful. They paid me for it. Deep down, I didn't feel right about it, but I kept on doing it, convincing myself maybe that it was "just for fun." Then one day, someone came to me and wanted me to read her teacup. I could tell right away that she was a bit disturbed, and I felt a bit uneasy. I looked into her teacup and saw my grandmother's face. I was so frightened. She urged me on, and I looked again, and saw my grandmother's face again! I told her I just couldn't do it, and she wanted to pay me even more money. I refused all of her money and gently told her I just wasn't able to do this anymore. I never, ever read another teacup.

My grandmother was a Christian woman and she was very strong. I was fortunate to have a Christian grandmother. She was supportive. She said, "With what you have been through, you could have been an angry woman, or a drunken woman." I had the potential to become a drinker. I know this is true.

I was saved by my faith. I knew I was loved. I didn't have to prove anything to anyone. I knew God saw me for what I was, for who I was. My children were approaching their teens and beginning to get into some drinking. I was worried about them. I made up my mind and I just turned around. I joined AL-ANON [the organization that helps parents and spouses of drinkers] to try to get some help for myself. I then began to work really hard in AL-ANON, to help me understand. I was worried about my children. I used to stay awake nights worrying if they would hurt themselves, or if they would possibly leave a cigarette burning accidentally, and I would lose the house. I was afraid of so many things, and really had to learn to let those worries go. I had to trust. AL-ANON taught me to trust.

In the past, everything had been taken from me, and lost, or we'd been evicted. Here, I had complete control of everything, and I wanted to make sure it wasn't taken away.

My work at the hospital was as a "float." My shift started at 7:00 a.m. I'd call the children at eight o'clock to wake them. Sometimes, they'd answer the phone, and go back to bed. They'd be late for school. One day, the school principal, social worker, the administrator of the hospital, my supervisor, and I met. They told me my kids were missing too many school days, that I should go on welfare. I said, "I don't want to go on welfare." I started to cry. I asked to change my shift at the hospital, but they said they couldn't. They said the only other shifts they had were evening shifts, and that wouldn't be any better.

I was forced on welfare then. I felt my dignity was stripped, as it had been when I had my beads taken and my braids cut at residential school. I felt brokenness again.

One day, after the kids went to school, I had an idea. I owed money. I had a bill to pay, and so I called and asked if I could pay off the bill by doing housework. The people were really happy with my work, and so asked me back the next week. In no time,

I was earning $20 to $30 a day doing housework. I had to report this to welfare and turn it in, but it just felt so good to be working. It felt good to leave home to go to a job and then to go back home again. I remember the satisfaction it gave me to clean and shine a hardwood floor.

After a while, I had a new [social] worker who said, "You're the kind of person we want to help. Whatever you earn, you keep." I was careful with money. I joined a parents-without-partners group, and we exchanged children's clothing. I had a strong mother who taught me that I could do everything for myself. It was especially difficult being on welfare, but I told myself, "This too, will pass." I told myself, "Better things will happen."

New Life

Over time, Gladys established herself as a reliable worker in the town of Portage la Prairie. Then, she experienced a gift of new life and happiness. She met a man who brought a deep love that she had not previously experienced. His gentleness and deep respect for her as well as for her children had a profound impact.

For Gladys, after being treated brutally by many men, this relationship was a positive one, a life-giving one that brought much joy. Her self-esteem grew, and after some years, the relationship brought the additional joy of new life in the birth of her youngest son.

This was a relationship which was just meant to be. It was not an experience I thought I would ever have in my life. The relationship and the birth gave me a second chance to heal.

I really appreciate this saying by Deepak Chopra: "There are some things that require no work, and healing is one of them. You don't have to work to achieve a silent mind; you don't have to work to find the old wounds. All these things are a given, once they are uncovered. The uncovering begins wherever you are now. But its goal is always the same—the revelation of wholeness that unites mind, body and spirit as one."[2]

We begin where we are now. By this time in my life, I had learned to be an individual. I had found my goals. My goals are always the same. I wanted to be happy, and to me, mind, body, and spirit are one. This is what my Dakota tradition teaches. In the church, we are taught that Father, Son, and Holy Spirit are one. I believe these are similar concepts. We, too, are one in mind, body, and spirit. This saying from Chopra's book was very helpful because it seemed so similar to my tradition.

In some ways, I knew myself so much better because of this relationship. I felt more my own person. I made decisions on my own, making my own choices, taking my own chances. This baby brought our family together; he brought a whole new meaning.

The pregnancy was a blessing, and the birth was joyful. Her grandmother had once told her that to bring a child into the world "on one's own" was to perform a feat like a mighty warrior. She had not intended that the birth take place at home, but the time of night and the swiftness of the birth worked together so that she did, indeed, deliver this child on her own. Her son arrived very quickly, just after midnight:

I felt so tired. I realized my new baby boy was here. I cried and cried—I was so relieved and happy. I was proud and glad that all went well. I reflected on my mother—11 children born at home, one in the hospital, and dad had been her helper. I knew my grandmother was watching over me and was pleased.

Gladys reflects on the joy of the birth of her youngest; his birth was an affirmation of life, a miracle of love. At the birth, his father gave Gladys a gold ring with three pearls, one for each of her children. In the Dakota tradition, each child is a gift, and the ring reflected this giftedness, as well as his love for her and for the children.

The relationship ended, but the honest love and caring changed Gladys forever. She was able to have much more positive understandings with men after that. The gift of his love and care continues to uphold her.

Gladys continued to work in the local area, enjoying the opportunities for growth, enjoying the relationships with her children as they went to school, so different from the experience of alienation of her own childhood.

A special time for me was in the fall when the kids were getting ready for school. There was a real hustle and bustle with them getting ready for school. Having been in residential school and not having a family to be with at this time, made me appreciate this even more.

There was an excitement in the stories they came home from school with, in the meeting of new friends. I liked it when they left 10 minutes early to go and call on someone and walk together to school. I enjoyed my young son getting into band and music. Our house was so small that he couldn't practise his music at home, and so he'd go a whole hour early to school so he could practise. The effort he made to do well in his music was touching for me.

This brought happiness to me as a mother. There were so many surprises that brought closeness to the children. I know that an important part of building a strong character is harmony in one's home life, in one's family.

I remember a special Thanksgiving dinner. We had roasted deer meat and I made bannock. We had applesauce from the apple trees. Our vegetables all came from the garden. It was such a blessing, so majestic, because nothing was bought. Even our tea was muskeg tea. We call it swamp tea because we find it in wet areas. When I think of that Thanksgiving dinner, it showed how generous mother earth is. The blessing that was said didn't seem enough to me.

After being away for 18 years, my husband came to our home and asked if he could stay with us and be a family again. He was sober by then. At first, I wasn't sure. I asked the children, and they said, "Well, mom, if you feel that it would be all right for you." I prayed about it, and felt it was important to do. He stayed for 11 years. When he became ill with cancer, I looked after him. He recovered from cancer, but later died suddenly of a stroke when he had just turned 60.

When her husband died, Gladys' family arranged for his burial in the Anglican cemetery overlooking Sioux Valley.

When the federally assisted Native Alcohol and Drug Abuse Program began in Portage la Prairie in 1976, they asked Gladys to be coordinator. She was the most active person in the community doing healing work with people involved with substance abuse.

Gladys had rented a little house in Portage for 21 years. She had fixed it up as well as she was able to make it cozy and homey, but at times felt frustrated because it hadn't been kept up properly by the landlord. Finally, the day came when the house was condemned, and she was forced to move. After much searching, miraculously three days before she had to leave, the house next door became vacant.

I saw my neighbours moving out, and asked, "Where are you going?" They said they were moving, and I said I was looking for a house to rent. They asked if I wanted to rent it.

I was so happy. They said they would rent it for three months, then they would have to sell. Within three months, I had managed with my savings to make a down payment. I was finally able to own my own home! The timing couldn't have been better. As they were moving out the front, I was moving in the back. This was like a dream come true, having our own little house, and I could really fix it up and make it how we wanted it to be. My self-esteem took a really positive turn. This was such a spiritual thing. Our needs were taken care of. I was so happy to do this on my own, finally to have my own home.

God's Love

Communion has always been important for Gladys. A bishop from Brandon once visited her community when she was 14 or 15 years old. She recalls the profound impact his visit had. It was common for many people in the parish not to go for communion. When he recognized that they were not having their communion regularly, he set aside his sermon and talked to them about it.

I'll never forget the way he talked, with such love. He seemed to understand that the people somehow didn't feel "good enough" and that was why they weren't going for their communion. He called on all who were baptized to come up for communion, and he talked about God's love for them.

My mother went up, and we were able to take communion together after years of her not taking communion. For her, the problem was that she was living in a common-law relationship, and she felt this prevented her taking communion. From then on, we were all free to worship and to have communion together.

I have always gone to church. After moving to Portage la Prairie, for many years I sat at the back. I somehow didn't feel I was as good as everybody else. It was so hard to believe I had anything to offer. Then, one day something happened to make my Jesus become more real for me.

I was at a "Cursillo," a conference to learn about Christianity. One night, after we finished our program, we were going to communion. I was surrounded by a community of love—and I felt the care and support of the community. As we were going to the communion, they used the word *agape* and said that this special communion on that evening was called *agape*. What they meant by this was *love!* They meant the unconditional love of God.

But, the most amazing thing to me was that in my language, *agape* translated literally means 'bread'!

Suddenly, I could see that this "love" of God is also the nourishment of my life, my bread. Suddenly, I made a deep connection. I felt that God loved me. I felt valuable—just the way I was, just the way I am.

God—God is nourishing. My image of God had changed. I knew always about God. I think I knew about God mostly from Granny Anne. But, God was also described at residential school as a God who was watching to make sure you didn't step out of line. The old residential school image of God was negative, a God to be afraid of.

Suddenly, with this agape feast, I knew God to be a God of love and compassion. It was so profound to me. Communion bread meant the body of Christ and the communion connected in the Christian understanding and the Dakota understanding. I felt this overflowing love to be shared, and I had a different personal feeling taking communion then. I think that the people around me must have wondered what was wrong. I might have seemed stunned. I tried to explain, but I couldn't seem to, and then I thought, "Oh well, this is my precious moment."

Maybe in my heart I always knew about this unconditional love, but this new image, this bread coming together, was a deeper understanding of a God who loves and cares for me.

The next time I went to my church in Portage la Prairie, I marched up to the front of the church instead and sat there. Now, I always sit at the front of the church.

Insights in Healing

In her work with National Native Alcohol and Drug Abuse in Portage la Prairie, many people were referred to Gladys through the courts, child welfare agencies, and social services. She began to be more and more respected as a counsellor and advocate for Native peoples. Many people also sought help from her voluntarily. After about 10 years of counselling Native people, Gladys began to realize that a lot of people who came to her with alcohol and substance abuse problems had been sexually abused. She found it frightening. She sensed they wanted to talk about it, but she felt inadequate, didn't know how to help them. Then, one day a crisis occurred at work that caused her to begin to deal with the abuse she had been subjected to as a child.

A man had been referred to me with a drinking problem, and so I saw him and counselled him over a number of weeks. Then, he came to me with another problem. He confessed he had raped his sister-in-law, and he wanted me to help him deal with this. I got up and walked away. I told him he would have to leave. I was so sick.

Then, I felt terrible about turning him away. To watch him walk away was so difficult. He had his cap in his hand. He took his cap, and slowly raised it, and then he dropped it. He looked at me, and his eyes were so pleading. He got up so slowly. What really moved me was that as he walked away, he looked so defeated.

I said to him, "Just a minute, maybe we can work something out." I couldn't let him go. His steps coming back were a lot faster than his steps going away. I got a coffee for both of us, and sat down with him. Just as quickly I told him, "I don't know how I'll be able to help you, but I'll have to pray. We'll pray to the Great Spirit for some help." So, I held both his hands, and we prayed together.

That was the beginning of becoming more aware of my own pain. I could identify with the helplessness he had expressed. I could see myself many times walking away with very heavy feet and a heavy heart. Something came together for us there in that prayer. It was like two helpless people, the blind leading the blind.

Somehow I was strong enough to sit there listening to his story. At the same time, I felt a lot of hate and pain for what he did. But, I couldn't turn away from someone who called for help, and so that was another new beginning.

Together we worked out a plan for him to get some help. A few days later I called my supervisor and told him I really needed to get some training. Within a week I was able to attend training on sexual abuse in San Jose, California. It was there that I "relived" the abuse. It was the beginning of really dealing with all the sexual abuse. While I was there, I was given the names of two therapists in Winnipeg who could help me, and went into therapy for several years.

It seemed for a while as though there was a part of me who was a little girl, quite separate from me. She was ugly to me. I had to tell her she was beautiful. She was beautiful then and she is beautiful now. I didn't know about the inner child until I was in therapy. I had left her when she got raped because that was when all the trouble started. During therapy it was some time before I could even include this inner child into my life in today's living.

I thought of what a smart little girl she was, and how much fun she was, laughing and playing. She was fun to be with, and then I started to feel sorry for her. But, it didn't come easy. It took a long time. But, the best part for me was when I connected to her and felt she was pretty. She wasn't ugly at all. What had happened to her was ugly.

I had felt it a godsend sometimes that I have so many good friends, so many people good to me, but I couldn't face my own memories until then because they hurt. I was almost a victim of my memories until that connection came.

It's the little girl part of myself that had to be loved, to know she was loved and a part of me. I feel that she is almost a playful part of me, and she's with me now. She's a happy part of me now, because she's come alive! She's joined the living.

FORGIVENESS

When I first began to heal, I talked to anyone who would listen. Then, I was stopped by someone who said it made her feel awkward. It was then that I understood that there are certain people we can go to, and where we are able to share, and that there are other times and other places one shouldn't or can't share. Later on, I understood how hard it is sometimes to listen to someone talking of their pain. I found this difficult, even with my own daughter.

At that time, I saw immediately with my own children that they reacted in anger. They wanted to strike out, to lash out against the people who had hurt me. I remember especially in 1991 at a reunion of Elkhorn School, that a meeting occurred which was excruciatingly painful.

Her children had joined Gladys at the reunion for the church worship service and communion. Leaving the church, she saw directly in front of her the man who had raped her over 50 years before. He was now elderly. Together with the children, she walked over to him and introduced them to him.

The man smiled and started to say I was a good girl, then I saw he had remembered. I could feel my whole body tightening up. We turned and started to walk away, but I sensed there was something left undone. I went back. I put my hand out, and he gave me his hand. I said, "I forgive you." Then I just turned around and joined my children. I was shaking so and I felt I wanted to throw up. I grabbed them one on each side of me. I just held their arms, as though I was hanging on for my life as we walked.

They said, "What's the matter, mom?" I said, "Let's get into the car." Then, I told them, "That's one of the men who raped me." Then I broke down. We were all crying. It was a terrible moment for them because I hadn't told them anything about it before. They held me. All of a sudden, I felt calm and looked around, looked at them and said, "Don't cry for me anymore. Help me heal. I have to heal. Help me heal.

From then on, I've moved on with life. I've had moments, lots of moments of sadness. Sometimes I can't believe what I've been through, but it brought a lot of peace of mind for me. Also, it brought me closer to my children.

This was the first time they knew about the rapes. My son told me later he wanted to go back and kill the guy. My daughter was filled with anger, anger and rage. "How did you ever raise us?" she asked. And suddenly she understood more about me, about the kind of parent I was. I raised them the way I was raised in school.

Perhaps the most painful thing for me still is the loss I feel in the relationships with my children as they were growing up. I was so authoritarian, because that was how I thought I had to be.

I felt I couldn't show love the way I would have wanted to. It was the only way I knew how to be with my children for a long time, until I recovered more and more of my own tradition.

This was true not only with my children but with others as well. I held back because I didn't want to be rejected, or made fun of. Often, I didn't want to take too much risk. I often didn't want people to know me too much.

But there always seems to be a way to get through if we can only stay with the positive as my mother told me to do. In my memory, I often went back to the one person who really showed me something of the love of God in those school days. Sometimes when I would ask my son to do something, like join events or activities in school, he would ask, "Why?" and I would say, "Because Granny Anne said that was the right thing to do!" I wanted him to take advantage of all the opportunities that came his way, because it is only in doing this he would find out his own capabilities.

"Who's Granny Anne?" he'd ask.

I explained to him that Granny Anne was the most trusting and encouraging person at the school. She always made us feel good about ourselves. She was a positive memory that kept me going. When I was starting to heal later, the positive memories started to connect, and I remembered the love of Granny Anne. Instead of becoming a victim of my memories, I started to connect with the good. I felt so bad. To think negatively was to put myself back into that kind of negative perspective. Granny Anne did so many things with us. She taught us how to work with our hands. She helped us in putting our crafts into the fair, and getting prizes for our hard work.

For a long time I lost track of Granny Anne. Then, when she was celebrating her hundredth birthday, her daughter-in-law let me know that she had said she would like to see me. I was so excited. I flew with my son to Vancouver. I could see that she was [happy] too! At first she didn't recognize me. Then I smiled and she said, "That's my Gladys!" Since then, her family has become like an extended family to me. I can still see her, the way she smiled.

I feel now as though I have now met so many people like Granny Anne. I meet more and more all the time.

We are much closer now. My children have helped me to heal. My first daughter, who wasn't part of our lives for many years, has now become a part of our family as well. Together with her own daughter, she visits us.

For a long time, I seemed to be connected in a deep way to the culture, but without knowing how to help in beadwork and making of traditional costumes. But my children had enough of the culture that they could take the next step. My daughter learned to bead and to make their traditional outfits for dancing. My daughter and grandchildren are all dancers and so we have a wonderful time going to pow-wows and traditional ceremonies camping together. They continue to practise the teachings of our culture. They keep sweetgrass in their homes, our native plant that we use for purification. They honour the traditional ways.

Reconnecting with Cultural Traditions

When I began to heal, I knew that the teachings of my culture would help me. I spent more time with my natural father. Although I had begun to lose my language, over the years I've understood that I had a lot of teaching as well. I am still closest to Hazel and Doreen, my sisters. Hazel has become a teacher, and Doreen became a community health worker in Sioux Valley, and we still help each other out. They are both retired now, but they are both still very active, Hazel in gardening, and Doreen in sewing and quilting.

I understand more and more that spirituality is evident in all parts of our lives. Those of us who are Native have our culture with us every day. Spirituality is always so evident in all of life. I look at birds and trees, I look at flowers, the buds, the new life and growth, and see God's work in everything.

For me, I can pray everywhere. The world, and all in it, is our altar. Mother earth is all around. To me, the Sundance for Dakota people is parallel to being confirmed. We make a commitment when we are confirmed, and the commitment of my sister to the Sundance is a similar commitment. Time is made for visitors to approach the sacred tree and pray for healing of illnesses. What is done here is to me like what we do in Christian services and call "communion of saints" which you never let go of, or forget.

I don't go inside the Sundance or participate. I don't talk about what participants do inside the Sundance out of respect. I believe participants feel strongly about the Sundance in the way I feel strongly about my communion. I miss my communion if I go too long without it. It doesn't matter where I am, in what province or city, I'm always directed to a church where I can have my communion, especially when so far from home. It always gives me a sense of peace. It is wonderful when people join in unity in God's sight. Where ever you go, you find this. It is everywhere.

I couldn't see this before. I thought one had to just stay in one's own little family. But now I see with the family of God, we are part of others all over the world. God is everywhere. This is the idea, to learn to accept this. Family is very important in our culture. There is a hidden law: we simply understood that we would be taken care of. Extended family take care of each other

I used to sit in class sometimes and watch the birds land in the trees. It was almost as though the birds were looking straight at me. I would think, "Oh, the bird is bringing me a message from my mother." It was as though the bird was telling me that she was fine and she loved me. I would say, "Okay, thank you for the message!" and then the bird would fly away!

It was a great loss when my mother died in 1970. Since that time, however, I've had a close relationship with my natural father.

I am so glad to have a close relationship to my children. When my son told me he was really in love, I gave him the ring my mother-in-law had given me years before, when I was leaving Yankton with the children. The ring was a symbol of her love for me. She said, "I want you to have this ring because I love you." I understood that there was a powerful love symbolized by the ring.

I prayed over the ring before giving it to him, praying that somehow the ring would be a positive help to their relationship, and take away any anxiety. At first, I thought he might prefer something brand new. Possibly he thought she would be disappointed that it was an "old" ring. But, I explained to him how much it meant to me when my mother-in-law had given it to me. His fiancee really loved it, and it was special that he was able to give it to her, to share this symbol of love.

Their relationship is a cross-cultural relationship, and they do have to deal with the differences between cultures. This, they will manage because of their love for each other. The ring brought us all together.

Our Life Path

Over time, in her work, Gladys has worked hard to reconnect with the teachings of the Dakota. In finding her own path, she has also prepared a path for others to follow. In bringing healing, Gladys affirms both Native and Christian traditions.

I have a friend who is a minister. He asked me once to help at Thanksgiving, to explain it in the Native way. I was glad to do this, but I also had to say that in our understanding, our "thanksgiving" is every day of our life. Every day we are to give thanks. In our lives, on our paths, we sometimes make mistakes, but then we are able to make corrections. There is hope and there is forgiveness.

Of all ages, at our age we must learn from the young. The young make us think in ways which call us to make positive and fair decisions. Young people need to connect with older people, because older people have lived through a lot of experiences. We need to find a balance between the old and the young.

[With] the help of my father, with the encouragement of my children, I have searched for and rebuilt what I need to live in this world. We have to be honest and yet share the knowledge we have learned because they [young people] may need it.

We must above all let children know they are spiritual beings and let them know we care for them. Sometimes we're so busy looking after daily chores, we forget to tell them that. We sometimes think they just know that we love them without our saying it. As they grow, we need to respect their choices, even when we may disagree with them. We must always keep the door open to our children and grandchildren.

The drum symbolizes the heartbeat of our mother and offers us comfort and direction all our lives. That's why we have a good feeling when we go to pow-wows. When we hear the drum, it brings us together as part of a big family, and we are all close to our own mothers and mother earth.

Honour is expressed in the making of the star blanket. The star blanket is really important in our culture. The blanket is usually given in return for a kindness shown by a friend or a relative. It is a high honour to receive a blanket. The burst on the star blanket is recognized as growth outwards, with the colours going from lighter to darker shades. As the colours grow darker, the feelings of deep respect, honour, and friendship for the person receiving the blanket get stronger. These colours are usually chosen by the blanket maker in accordance with the feelings they hold for the receiver. The individual ray's growth, coupled with the colour progression into darker shades, represents the continuous addition of people cared for and remembered.

Star blankets are given at births, as well as deaths and celebrations of thanks. Teachings about the star blanket and many other traditions of our culture weren't written. Everything was taught through words, but the words were very carefully chosen. We had lots of important teachings. Life is a journey, and we have the chance to keep learning and growing.

The Wind of God

Once, I went back to my husband's people, the Lakota people. I had heard about the sacred pipe ceremony. I went with my sister.

The sacred pipe, the symbol of deep communion, is used on very special occasions. It is shared only in certain ways. The most honoured and trusted people become carriers of the pipe. They are the wise ones of the community.

When the pipe is to be used, it is brought to the ceremony in a procession. We were there in the hills of South Dakota when suddenly, the procession appeared over a hill. I could see in the distance a young maiden on a white horse at the head of the procession. She was dressed in a white buckskin with long fringes and beautiful beadwork. There was a sense of majesty about the procession. In her hand was held the sacred pipe bundle wrapped in buffalo skin.

She was surrounded by four maidens walking on four sides of the white horse; they in turn were surrounded by honorary guards. The procession was led by a medicine man in full traditional dress. The medicine man is honoured in the community.

Ahead of the procession, people spread sage on the ground for the procession. Sage is a kind of sweetgrass, a medicine to Native people.

I remembered so clearly the passage about Jesus riding into Jerusalem on a donkey, and the people were putting palm branches on the ground ahead of him. I watched how the people picked up the sage after the procession had passed by. First some came, and then others and then others until the pathway was completely clear behind the procession.

Then, I told my sister that I would go back to the path. It was hot and I had a hat with me. As I went back to the path, suddenly a wind came. I knew that wind was the breath of God!

My hat came off. I didn't even look to see where it was. I didn't want to spoil the moment. I stood there beside the path not thinking about the path or about the people around me. It was as though I was all alone and God was with me and had touched me. He blessed me in that gentle touch of the wind on my face.

This is what helped me to heal, support from my children and family. Granny Anne and my mother were no longer with me, but I had my children and father and sister to listen to me. There were others; I had therapists trained to help. I had to learn to ask for help.

It was such a heavy load for me when I first started to open up. The load kept getting lighter and lighter. Love overflowed from the hearts of people who helped me. They were like shining stars, my children, my family, my father, and others who helped.

The faith I had became stronger and helped to make me well. My faith was with me all the time, but I had to put it to work. When there was no one else to talk to, I talked to God. When I wanted to heal, my whole life changed. I knew God was leading me, and I wasn't alone.

It was like coming out of the darkness into light, being born again, this time into a deeper understanding of God's love.

Unconditional Love

Not long ago, one of my friends gave me a book of poems by Helen Steiner Rice. I love poetry, and she knew that. That was part of the reason she gave me the gift. But, there was another reason. She gave me the book because she really cares about me. She was concerned about my health. I have diabetes, and I have to watch my diet. When she gave me the book, she was also offering to help me to watch my diet, to care for myself more, because she really doesn't want to "lose me," she said.

I was so deeply touched by this. It is hard for me to explain how very touched I was. She was non-Native. She was a long-time friend, and she was concerned about me. I knew God put her in my life. Sometimes, when I needed her, that's when she would come with a big hug. It has been so easy for us to pick up the phone and talk to each other. She made a special effort to come and see me, and the love she demonstrated was "no big deal," it was just there.

This is unconditional love in the truest form, a love where there are no questions asked, just true caring. I looked at the cover of the book. There was a beautiful rose on the cover, and I put my finger on the picture of the rose. I understand somehow that when I touch the petals of this flower, I connect with the flower itself. Through the flower, I connect with roots, I connect with mother earth, and with the universe. Everything is universal; I can connect with anything, anywhere. I am connected with my own person, and I am connected with everything, everywhere.

It is this understanding which makes it possible for me to care for others, to look after others. It is this understanding which helps me to understand that I myself am cared for. People express this to me sometimes, as my friend did.

I also I know that somewhere, somewhere deep within, I understand that I am loved, deeply loved with an unconditional love by our Creator.

Gladys continues to work with the National Native Alcohol and Drug Abuse Program in Portage la Prairie, and volunteers as well. She has a special interest in youth, and works tirelessly on women's concerns. She has been honoured by receiving the Premier's Award for volunteer work, and numerous other awards for community service. In October 1996 she received the Governor General's Award for promoting women's rights.

In the First Nations community, she is called on frequently to serve as elder, and serves on the National Council of Elders. She has twice been gifted with a sacred pipe. To be a "pipe carrier" is a very great honour.

She is active in her parish and recently received the Order of Rupert's Land for contributions to her diocesan community. She served on the Residential Schools Working Unit and was featured in an award-winning film, *Search for Healing*. She continues to serve on the Anglican Council of Indigenous Peoples.

Vi Smith

Edited by Joyce Carlson

Vi Smith was born on January 19, 1916, in the dead of winter, in the village of Gitanmaax. The village had been undisturbed until the arrival of the first white person in 1832, only 84 years before. Vi has been active in her local parish of St. Peter's in the village of Hazelton, in the Diocese of Caledonia, and in the national Anglican Church of Canada as Leading Elder of the Anglican Council of Indigenous Peoples. The daughter of a hereditary chief in a matrilineal West Coast society, the person we know as Vi Smith has quite a different identity within her own community:

I am Wii Bistaii of the Gisgaast clan, in the house of Dowamuux of the Gitksan Nation. We live in our territories in what is now known as northern British Columbia. Our river is the Xsan. It is known as the Skeena because early explorers who came to this country couldn't pronounce our words.

We are a matrilineal society. The robes I wear embody the spirit and strength of my mother, my maternal grandmother, and my maternal aunts and uncles. We are surrounded by the Nations of the Wet'suwet'en, the Nishga'a, the Tsimshians, and the Taltans, also known as the Stikine.

There is a common thread of understanding of all created life between our Gitksan and other First Nations across Canada. Our own philosophy or belief is that all life forms are equal, necessary, and to be respected. Today, the belief has not changed, but some of us do not practise the belief fully. Our forebears allowed a European culture, through the government and the church, to "civilize" us, we know now, in exchange for our territories and resources.

In Genesis 16, we read the story of Sarai and Abram. Sarai was unable to produce an heir. She had a young Egyptian slave girl named Hagar. Sarai gave Hagar to Abram as a concubine, so that Hagar could produce an heir for Abram. Scripture tells us that Hagar became pregnant.

My problem with the story is the disregard of Hagar's feelings as a person, a part of God's creation. Was Hagar consulted or asked if she wanted to bed with Abram? Pregnant and hated by Sarai, treated cruelly, she ran away. Ishmael heard the distress of Hagar; there had been no regard for her feelings as a mother, as a person. Yes, Hagar was a slave, but still a human being. Sarai and Abram were the important ones. Hagar, a part of God's creation, was excluded.

Being a mother, I can relate to Hagar rather than Sarai. There are other similar stories in the Old Testament. In the story of Esther, Queen Vashti is cast aside because she refused to satisfy the whims and fears and pride of her husband.

With the colonization process, we have become numbers. We have lost the sacredness of creation. The governments have tried to take away our identity, our distinctiveness, and our language. They almost succeeded.

From the beginning, we have learned about you, your cultures, your ways of thinking, your beliefs. We have listened to you. Until lately, we have not talked to you about us. We have not shared ourselves, our history from our perspective. You were not ready to listen to us.

Hear us now.[3]

People of the Mist

Gitanmaax Village is inland from the Pacific coast about 250 kilometres along the mighty Xsan, 'river of the mists.' Mists rise from churning waters in ever-changing patterns up the mountainsides, particularly in winter. Vi's ancestors called themselves the Gitksan, 'people of the mist,' after their beautiful river. Early coastal explorers, however, found the river swift and treacherous, so avoided travel inland.

Because of the mildness of the winter, furs weren't as desirable as in eastern Canada. The first European traders moved in only when animals were becoming scarce in eastern Canada and the prairies in the early 1800s. Until then, the people lived as they had since the glaciers melted creating a flood some 10,000 years before. Their stories tell of 'the time after the flood.' The lush rain forests, warmed by the Japanese currents of the Pacific Ocean, are one of the richest natural environments in the world. Wildlife and game were abundant everywhere. Berries grew along rivers and mountainsides. The river supplied their staple food, the salmon. Methods of fishing were so sophisticated and well developed that even now they are used by commercial fishers. The skill of the Gitksan in preserving and storing meant that most food for the year was harvested in the summer.

The richness of the natural environment allowed Gitksan peoples to provide quite easily for their basic needs and to live in semi-permanent villages. Gitanmaax means 'people who harvest fish with torches' because the villagers developed a unique fishing method; they shone torches above the ice to attract fish and caught them in nets. Gitanmaax, the village of Vi's father, is located at the junction of the Xsan and the Bulkley rivers. Vi's mother was from a nearby village called Anspayaxw, 'the place where one hides,' located strategically at a part of the Xsan where people could hide from possible attack.

These villages were located only a few kilometres apart along the river, and visiting and intermarriage between them were common. Linguistically a part of the Tsimshian language group, the Gitksan, like neighbouring Nations, had a well-developed social structure.

The primary political unit was the house, named after village longhouses in which my ancestors lived at one time. House members shared a common ancestry, a common oral history, reflected in songs, and crests which are carved on household items and poles and incorporated in ceremonial regalia. People's responsibilities to each other and to the natural world were carried out through the head chief of the house. The head chief acted in consultation with a number of other chiefs, called "wings" of the head chief, as well as with elders. On larger matters, he consulted as well with chiefs of other houses.

Persons were born into the mother's house, and succession to names came through the mother's side. Closely related houses remained close to each other; the chiefs of these houses consulted frequently with each other. The broadest grouping of related houses was the clan. In Gitksan society those clans were: Fireweed, Wolf, Frog, and Eagle. Members of the same clan were forbidden to marry.

In this matrilineal society, the father's house was also important, particularly in the beginning and end of life. A father had responsibility to raise his children well, although they never became members of his own house or clan unless adopted into it for reasons such as extension of the father's house. Throughout their lives, children were expected to reciprocate the care they received from their father. At death the father's house arranged the burial. This is still in effect.

Through clans, people had connections with neighbouring societies. Kinship networks extended throughout the whole region. In travelling, people recognized their kin through totem poles displayed in front of houses.

> Each village consisted of a cluster of longhouses built of cedar, which grew abundantly in the rain forests. Longhouses were about 40 feet (12.5 metres) wide, and 40 to 100 feet (12.5 to 31 metres) long and 10 to 14 feet (3 to 4.5 metres) high. In these multigenerational dwellings, each family had a particular place, with individual cooking hearth, sleeping benches, and storage areas. Fish, smoked in specially built smokehouses, as well as dried berries and fruit were stored in boxes or baskets under the rafters of the longhouses.
>
> The village of Anspayaxw where Vi's mother was born and the village of Gitanmaax ('people of the raven') where her father was born are only 16 kilometres apart along the Xsan. Vi's father, a member of the Frog clan, was known as Gademgald'o, 'man from the deep woods.' Vi's mother, of the Fireweed clan, took on the name of her own mother, and the name of her house, Dowamuux, 'frozen ear.'
>
> Names were part of a web of relationships and identified place in community, and connection to territory.

The special relationship between the people and their territories can best be expressed as a covenant with inherited responsibilities. Leaders, whose responsibilities included care of the territories, were chosen by the people of the house. They were trained by the people and trusted by the people. The decisions and actions of leaders were judged by contributions to "the good of the community." In effect, the people were as secure as the strength, character, and knowledge of their leader.

The land was constant and relationships were connected to the territories through a matrilineal system which provided crest, clan, name, song, protection, and privilege to all within the house, as well as others given special status or rights. For example, a person might be given the privilege of using the territory of a spouse as long as the link of marriage in the house remained. If a marriage ended, the person's privilege also ended. The economic security of children was assured through rightful and privileged use of two territories, the mother's and the father's. The relationship between women and men was given dignity and equality because women held title, property rights, and personal interests in their own matrilineal line from birth to death. The boundaries of territories were identified and confirmed by neighbouring authorities through the feast system. The relationship of people to the land was rooted in their understanding of covenant responsibility to the land and to all of life sustained by the land. This covenant rested in a belief in the truth that all created life forms are equal and necessary for harmony and survival of the whole.

We believe that the Creator gave us the land. We were born with the spirit of the land. In the same way, in our understanding, we were born with our territories. *Adakw*, our oral history, tells us our territory. The territory of my extended family has been passed down to my grandmother, my mother, and to my brother, my sister, and me. My children and my sister's children inherit this land. My brother's children inherit the territory of their mother's house, but throughout his life, he remains a part of his own mother's house.

> Winter was the time for feasting, storytelling, visiting, and making of utensils and clothing. The identity of each member of Gitksan society was reflected in the stories and songs, as well as in the symbols carved on totems and utensils. Even the most basic household utensils were finely made and, often, elaborately carved. Gitksan men were, and continue to be, master carvers. The bentwood box used for storing foods, transporting items by canoe, as well as for carrying berries is made of a single cedar plank steamed and bent by skilled woodworkers to form sides. Cedar is a

wonderfully strong yet soft wood containing natural oils that prevent decay. The size of the box depended on its use. They were used for storing domestic items, implements, and tools. With hot stones placed inside, the boxes could be used for cooking. At ceremonial feasts, they were used as drums. At the end of life they were used for cremation.

One of the ancient skills of the women was weaving. They also used cedar for their daily garments. They wove the inner bark of the red cedar with mountain goat wool, collected in summer, to create beautiful cloaks, coats, and blankets that shielded against the damp and the cold of winter.

Special regalia worn at feasts and other special occasions was woven from goat hair and cedar bark in intricate patterns and with crests. After the Europeans arrived, robes were more commonly made of wool blankets with mother-of-pearl buttons. The blankets were usually navy or black with red trim, beautifully patterned with crests and symbols and buttons. They were handed down in families. The regalia given to Vi by her mother and grandmother is an example of this adaptation.

The Arrival of the Europeans

In my family, some of the impact of the arrival of new-comers was deeply felt. My paternal grandfather had been a well-known and respected factor of a Hudson's Bay Post. When he left the community, it would have been impossible for either my grandmother, or the child born of the union, my father, to leave. Although he left my grandmother and father, Charles Clifford remained in Canada and lived in Victoria. He invited my father to come to Victoria when he was older to get an education. My father's uncle later refused to allow my father to accept the invitation to go to Victoria for education. The fear was that he might choose not to return.

My father was an important person in his family and community, a potential chief in the house of his mother. The vision the family had for him was borne out in his life. He became chief in his own house. This made him eligible for the position of head chief of Gitanmaax. When he became chief, he was given the name Gademgald'o at a special feast ceremony. Within my family there are a number of names held by the person before working up to the head name.

A Gitksan Childhood

Gademgald'o and Dowamuux, respected names within the community, were not acknowledged by church and government. Vi's parents were known as Charles and Mabel Clifford, after Charles' British father. Vi was baptized Violet Mary Clifford; she was also given a child's name from within the house of Dowamuux. Charles' mother, sister of the head chief of Gitanmaax, was known as Rose Mowatt.

Vi's grandmother was known as Lucy to outsiders. A *halayt*, she was recognized in her community for her gift of healing. *Halayt* literally means 'one who blows away evil spirits.' She continued as a healer in her own tradition until her death in 1940.

In the first generations of contact the people continued to carry names within house and territory, and there was little impact on the social structure. Surrounded by the physical world out of which the stories and legends of her people grew, Vi was steeped in Gitksan culture. She describes how the culture was imparted.

Many years ago, when our ancestors lived in longhouses, they lived with many families together. On a winter evening an elder would sit at the centre of the house and tell stories. The children would gather around close to the fire and listen. The story could go on and on. Sometimes the children would fall asleep, and if they did, that was okay. They would hear the same story again and again over the course of the next few years. They would have many opportunities to hear any part they may have missed.

While the children were cared for in this way by an elder, the parents could be clearing up after supper or working on carving, weaving, or mending nets. If a young couple were having marriage problems, the story might speak to them. A person of any age might pick up something important from the story.

As experience and understanding grew, so did the power and guidance of the legend's message. Oral legends were, and continue to be, important to the order and quality of Gitksan life. Storytellers, usually elders, become philosophers, historians, educators, psychologists, and memory holders. Storytellers are culturally obligated to give stories away. With every telling, listeners acquire more experience to appreciate lessons of the story. With every telling, the storyteller also adds more understanding to his or her own wisdom. The final step is for listeners to be mature enough to become storytellers themselves. This involves a "walking through" the experience of understanding self.

In Gitksan understanding, each person perceives truth when mind and spirit reach an appropriate level of understanding. Legends should only be told by such a person. More than words or drama, legends are free gifts of experience and knowledge. Cast out like seeds, legends can be dormant until triggered to growth by need and circumstance. They flow freely from one generation to the next, carrying beliefs, experiences, and traditions.

There are many different kinds of legends, but all have a specific purpose to guide, inform, and entertain. Some legends stand as legal documents and are considered the property of the house that holds territory validated in the legend. In this case, only a leader of a house, or his designated speaker, has the right to tell such a legend. Legends deal with human conditions: self-control, honesty, greed, deviant behaviour, responsibility, spiritual understanding, morality, etiquette, and ethics. In so doing, they uphold truth, reason, recognition of reality, honour, and respect.

One of the first stories Vi's mother told is about the mountain named on maps Rocher de Boule but known to the Gitksan as Stekyoodinahl, 'mountain of the rolling rocks.' The legend is called The Mountain Goats of Damlaxam:

In the time after the flood there was a big village in a clearing called Damlaxam where all the Gitsxan people lived. This clearing, a big field with no trees, was along the side of Stekyoodinahl mountain meaning 'rolling rocks' along the Xsan River. This is how the mountain came to be known as rolling rocks.

One day, after their hunting, the men of the village brought home a young goat. The children of the village made fun of the goat; they teased it and tormented it, putting a red colouring called ochre around its eyes. There was a young boy who lived in the village. When the other children abandoned the goat after tormenting it, this young boy went back to the goat to try to help it to heal. As he was helping the goat, he told it that the other children were mean, but that not everyone felt that way about him. When the goat was healed, he freed it and sent it back up the mountain to its home.

One day, four people came to the village in goat masks to invite the people to a great feast in their home up the mountain. All of the people except the very old and the very young children went up the mountain to this great feast.

When the people of the village arrived, they found that all the people who invited them had on great goat cloaks. The boy noticed that one of those in a goat cloak had red stains about his eyes. This was the very goat that the people had mistreated.

Then the feast began. In the middle of the feast, a great goat kicked down the beams of the feast hall. Suddenly there was a great rolling of rocks. When the goat retaliated in this way, everyone fell down a steep trail as the rocks rolled.

All the Gitksan people were buried by the landslide except the boy who had shown kindness to the goat.

The goat that he had protected kept him safe when the house was kicked down. Then, the goat told him which path to take to go safely down the mountain and back to his village. But when he saw how steep the path was, the boy was afraid he would slip and fall. The goat then took off his own small hoofs and gave them to the boy to wear down the mountain. This he did because he remembered the kindness of the young boy, which had helped him to heal and escape his tormentors. In this way the boy was able to find his way down the steep slopes. When he reached his village, he hung the small hoofs on a tree to give them back to the goat who came later to take them away.

The boy returned to his village and told the people what had happened, that everyone else had been killed because of the rocks rolling and sliding down the mountain. The only people remaining in the village of Damlaxan were the very old people who could not travel and the very young children.

My mother told me this story when I was very young. In the telling of the story, she was encouraging me never to make fun of animals because they are part of God's creation.

As a child, Vi camped summers with her family near Damlaxan. Everyone, including children, participated in gathering food and preparing for winter. The children learned by working with their parents. Berry picking was one of Vi's chores. In earlier days, berries were dried over open fires, wrapped in leaves, and stored in bentboxes. The women who were the weavers collected the wool of the mountain goats, roots, and cedar bark in the summer.

Throughout her childhood, stories were woven around everyday events to teach Vi. Her position as daughter of a hereditary chief required that she learn wisdom from an early age. The lessons were sometimes not easy for a young girl:

My mother and father lived a traditional way of life as much as they were able in those rapidly changing times. Although my father was half white, he was raised in the house of his mother's family, and trained in all the traditional wisdom to become a hereditary chief. This knowledge and wisdom was similarly shared with me as I was growing up. I was raised "a chief's daughter" with expectations for good behaviour that I sometimes found difficult. My mother always emphasized the need to be kind to all creatures, including other humans. I remember how she taught the important value of respecting and caring for others.

In the village there was a young man who was demented. When I was very young, we travelled to summer berry camps. Some people had wagons or buggies; my father hired a truck. In the evening, we placed the wagons and vehicles in a circle. With this camping arrangement, our families were very close together. It was clear that the mother of the young demented boy looked after the needs of all the others in her family first. We could hear him crying. To protect others, the boy waited to the back of their wagon.

When my mother was preparing food, she asked me to take food to this boy. Before feeding all of us, she prepared a plate for him. I was about 13 or 14 years old. The first time I was asked to take food to him, I did it without complaining. The second time I was asked to take food, I said I would be teased by my friends who said he was my boyfriend. I didn't want to do it, but I went ahead in spite of my protests because my mother had asked me. The third time, I refused outright. I told her someone else should go instead.

My mother replied, "Just do it because I asked you, and I'll explain why. This is an important lesson that I want you to learn, not your sister. Look into his eyes. He's a human being just like you and I. Therefore, you shouldn't treat him differently."

My mother wanted me to see beyond his deformity to his humanity. Since that time, it's been hard for me to laugh at anyone different from me.

Because of my identity as the daughter of a hereditary chief, I was given lots of affirmation, lots of positive encouragement. My parents made it clear that when they built up my self-esteem, it was not their intention for me to use it in negative ways.

The teaching of my mother is with me now. By having me look into the eyes of the young boy, she taught me, without saying it explicitly, not to make fun of others. To this day, I often hear elders advising "Don't make fun of people who are different."

Stories and legends, rooted as they are in the ancestral histories of the people, validate the presence of the people in their lands and describe their borders; they affirm extended family connections and outline authority and responsibilities.

The intricate relationship between the world of the people and the natural world is reflected in the origin stories. Different stories belonging to each house, family, and clan described particular relationships to the natural world. The masks, songs, and dance used to dramatically tell stories of ancestors and legends are also owned and passed down through families. In the stories and ceremonies the relatedness of creature to creation is reflected. An amazing gift of story is that it is adapted to the level of the listener.

While Vi's family and many others were doing their very best to teach Gitksan cultural traditions through stories, legends, and songs, the community around was undergoing rapid change. Missionaries had come to the community, and Vi's family were affected by this.

Being in northern British Columbia our people were one of the last across Canada to have contact with Europeans. At first, things didn't change, even though the traders and settlers moved in. They didn't try to change our lives. It was only when the missionaries came that they tried to change our way of thinking, our way of living.

There is an openness of the community to the understandings of others. People respected missionaries and priests because of the similarity of their beliefs. Although there may have been things wrong in the Christian faith which they didn't agree with, they were able to accept Christianity for the good they found. In the same way there may have been things wrong in our own traditions. The approach of my family was to take the good from both.

Some people within the community rejected Christianity because they felt the beliefs were another people's philosophy. My own parents accepted Christianity because they respected early missionaries. Gitksan were a people open to new ideas. Their integration of Christianity into our own traditions was a matter of doing what they thought was right, what they thought was best.

Vi's grandmother didn't accept Christianity but remained rooted in the ancient spirituality of the Gitksan. Her daughter, Mabel, Vi's mother, had begun attending church through a Methodist mission established in 1895 in the village of Anspayaxw.

My grandmother accepted my mother's decision to join the church out of respect. This is the way of our people. While she allowed her daughter's decision to be a part of the church, she was very strong in her own spirituality, and simply didn't acknowledge the presence of the church in her community. My parents were encouraged in the Christian faith through the guidance of a Roman Catholic priest. As there wasn't a Roman Catholic church in the village, the priest encouraged my mother and father to attend another church, saying, "It doesn't matter what church you attend as long as you become a Christian." They were most comfortable in the Anglican church in Hazelton.

Hazelton is a small European community adjacent to Gitanmaax. Vi's mother, like many other Gitksan women, hesitated to marry legally at first because of her fear that the patriarchal system would deny her rights as a Gitksan. This was a trying time for women. They struggled with what was right. They married in the traditional way first. Eventually, because the government didn't accept those marriages, and the church encouraged marriages, her parents were married in St. Peter's Church in Hazelton. Of the eight children born to them, three died in childhood. Vi was the third child, and was baptized at the age of seven into the Anglican faith.

Early Years in the Church

On Sundays, at the Anglican church, a morning service was in English. In the afternoon there was Sunday school as well as afternoon service with the Book of Common Prayer. Hymns were sung in English, scriptures were read in English and interpreted into Gitksan, and the sermon was always in Gitksan. The people had their own Church Army, and in the evening they gathered there, often late into the night, staying as long as they felt the presence of the Holy Spirit.

Both my parents were active in the Church Army. It was the more informal evangelical arm of the Anglican Church. There, people gave their own testimonies, and used an ordinary drum, and musical instruments like guitars, pianos, and clarinets.

Vi's father eventually served as a lay reader in the Church Army. St. Peter's stands on the banks of the 'river of mists,' below the ancient graveyard. Situated on a high cliff, the graveyard overlooks the river and the valley. Just below the church is a mighty totem, hand carved with crests and symbols of the house of Vi's father.

Vi's earliest memories are filled with Christian symbols side by side with Gitksan symbols. As well, her close and loving relationship with her mother kept her rooted in Gitksan cultural and spiritual traditions.

Vi's family lived in two cultures, making choices as best they could, trying to fit into what was becoming a dominant culture, while maintaining Gitksan identity.

Responding to Change

As long as they remained economically independent, and sovereign in their own territories, the people dealt with early traders and missionaries on their own terms.

Ethnologists affirm that West Coast cultures adapted amazingly well to early contact with Europeans. The first arrival of trade goods brought an accompanying flourishing of all the arts as people adapted their crafts to the increased variety of goods.

Thirty years after the arrival of the first white person, during the lives of Vi's grandparents, the smallpox epidemic of 1862 wiped out half of the population of the Gitksan in a single year. They had no immunity to smallpox, and the *halayt* could not treat it. In the words of ethnologists at the Royal British Columbia Museum, "One of the world's greatest tributes to the strength of the human spirit is that the people survived and remained sane through that terrible time."

It was in the time of Vi's great-grandparents that settlers began arriving.

When settlers came, they were welcomed, because part of our philosophy is that all life is equal. Our people saw human beings, they saw other lives. We had lots of land. At first, if a person came and said "I'd like to stay in your land," our ancestors would take them out, find a place by the river where the land was good. If the person built a cabin on that land, that was acceptable. It was only when the newcomers started to put fences around their cabins that Gitksan people started to wonder.

A great-grandfather in our house had a settler come visit him. They became friends. He took him to a choice piece of land and said, "You could stay here. There are lots of berries. You are close to the river where there are a lot of fish, and small animals in the valley close by. You could go up to the mountain and get the bigger animals." It was quite a distance from where he, my great-grandfather, was staying. So he didn't see the settler very often.

Once a year the settler would come and visit him. Then, after a while, he didn't come. My great-grandfather worried about him, saying, "I wonder if he's okay." He went to visit him. When he got there, there was a fence with a sign on it. My great-grandfather didn't know what was happening, so he didn't go in. He said, "I'd better go and find out why that fence is there." He saw a sign on the fence, copied it with what may have been charcoal, and took it with him.

Great-grandfather took the sign to a missionary doctor who had become very dear to the village people. Great-grandfather said, "What is this? I copied this from the fence that was built on my territory." The sign he read said "No trespassing." The doctor was a very kind man. We named our hospital after him. We call it Wrinch Memorial. He was a true Christian.

That was the beginning of our people wondering, "What is happening? Why are people building fences on our territory?"

At this point, the people became increasingly concerned as more and more settlers arrived. Vi's parents wished to help their children cope with the unprecedented change. Her father recognized that understandings of Gitksan culture alone would not be enough to assist his people. He had been offered education by his European father, but was not allowed to have it because of his position in the community. Vi muses:

My father made many decisions for us based upon his belief that we would need an education to deal with the many changes in the community. I sometimes wonder whether my father may have regretted the missed educational opportunity for himself. He and my mother emphasized the importance of education.

There has been a great appreciation for the church because education was started by the church before the government considered it important. People within the community believed education was important to help them to deal with outsiders and with the changes. I began formal schooling at the age of six and a half at St. Peter's day school. My first teacher was an Anglican priest. My next teacher was an Anglican lay woman, a kind soul.

Then Vi's parents chose to send Vi and her brother to a residential school. A third sibling attended a Roman Catholic school in a nearby community. Her parents carefully selected what they thought would be the best situation for each child, and were in a position to pay for travel for Vi and her brother, an amount of $70 each, a great sum in the 1920s.

It was my parents' decision to send me to residential school. When I was 10 years old, my parents decided the little school did not offer enough to prepare me to survive in what they considered a fast-changing world. There were several residential schools for Native children in B.C. established by the federal government and operated by churches.

My parents made inquiries as much as was possible at that time. They chose Coqualeelza Residential School situated in the Fraser Valley in Sardis. I had to travel by train to Prince Rupert, then by boat to Vancouver, then by tram to Sardis. To a 10-year-old, it was a great adventure!

It was a bit more painful for my parents to part with their 10-year-old child. I adapted to the ways and discipline of the school quite well, I think. Their ways and rules were similar to the ones at home. My parents were kind and loving, but strict in our upbringing. Most of the teachers at the school were kind and understanding. There were one or two I could have really lived without as they enjoyed their authority. You get these kinds of people in any school system.

The school was operated by the United Church, but once a month an Anglican Church priest came to the school to teach catechism to students who were Anglican. When I was 12 years old, I was confirmed at St. John's in Sardis.

I attended the residential school for five years, until I was 14. In retrospect, I feel the academic [level] was quite acceptable although one of the matrons was quite mean. One of her favourite sayings was "the very idea." I recall receiving a fairly severe beating after returning from a vaccination. I don't remember why.

There were other irritations associated with institutional life. We had figs and prunes for breakfast every day, and fish every Friday. I can laugh about this as an adult. I understand the nutritional need for fruit such as figs and prunes. My disappointment with the fish was that it wasn't cooked in the delicious way my mother cooked it.

To me, the real problem was we were not allowed to speak our own languages, or to speak to the boys. Of course, we did both. The trick was not to get caught. So, we learned to lie to protect ourselves.

Vi returned to Gitanmaax having completed grade 8. With her parents' encouragement, she enrolled in high school in Hazelton.

Hazelton had its own municipal offices and schools. The combined population of the two parts of the village in Vi's youth was only a few hundred, with about half being Gitksan and half other cultures. The high school Vi attended in Hazelton served European children. Vi was able to attend this school because her father was a friend of the local representative. She was the only student recognized by the government as Gitksan enrolled in the school.

The negative view of their culture was clear, especially to Vi's father, who had worked outside the community at different times, in pack trains, lumber camps, and sawmills. Quite a number of First Nations men worked in these areas. Because his father was European, his appearance was similar to the many French Canadian workers who also came to work in the area. First Nations peoples were often spoken of in negative terms, and so, at times, he simply allowed the people he worked for to believe he was French Canadian when they assumed that was his background. His own self-esteem never suffered.

Vi's mother, very dark and always recognized as Gitksan, said on occasion that she wished she were lighter. The external negative view of Gitksan culture was permeating the community. Vi recalls that most Gitksan used only the back door of the hospital and sat only on one side of the church.

There were deep hurts in her community caused by the racism and undervaluing of the spiritual traditions. Her own grandmother was a target of the police. She didn't feel she was doing anything wrong by using traditional medicines. However, the police had a great deal of power, and on one occasion when practising her healing, the house was forcibly entered by the provincial police, who confiscated her healing aids as well as her headdress. She was fortunate in not losing her robe, a very special part of her regalia, because it was at the home of Vi's mother when the police arrived. It was very hurtful to be treated in this way. In Vi's childhood, the police, whose word was respected in court over Gitksan, were feared by the Gitksan peoples. Her grandmother's sacred items have never been returned from the Museum of Civilization in Ottawa, in spite of requests.

The Land

Assumptions were made outside the community about the availability of land in the area without consultation or respect for our people. The government of British Columbia from its location in Victoria advertised land availability in English in the papers of many cities and towns. My ancestors were unable to read. Further, we live in northern British Columbia, far from where the publications are circulated.

The community spoke little English and were furious that others would presume to "claim" the land that was held in the trust of their families, houses, and clans. From the beginning of contact, they requested their territories be respected by newcomers. Their requests were not respected.

There is an intricate relationship between people and land. We are the land. The people are the land. We cannot separate ourselves from the land. It's not difficult for me to understand why the people of the Middle East refer to their land as holy. That's how we feel about our land. It is sacred.

In Gitksan culture, one can't talk about the land without talking about the spirituality and philosophy of the people. They cared for their territories to ensure a balance between human life and the created world, including plants and animals.

My dad cared for the land. He looked after my mother's land as well because my mom was at home nurturing the children and we were a big family. He would go to his lands up north and trap there for the season. If the trapping was good and the animals were plentiful, he'd go back next year. He seemed to know when the land needed [to] rest and to refurbish itself. At that time, he'd go to my mother's land.

Although he used my mother's land, he never ever claimed that land as his own. It remained my mother's, and everybody knew it was hers. He could only claim his own, and we, his children, couldn't claim his land. Our mother's land was our inheritance.

Every family had a territory and every territory had different parts. Each had a mountain; we needed the mountain for bigger animals. We had to have a valley for the smaller meats and the berries and the roots, for vegetables and for medicine. We had to have a piece of the river for our salmon; we are known as the salmon people. Salmon is very important to us, so the river is sacred.

The government has required us to register the land as "trapping land." This we do, much against our will but we do this in order to hold on to the land. The land registered as trapping land was much more than trapping to us. It was our way of life.

When people began to be concerned about their territories not being respected, they sent a delegation down to Victoria where the seat of the provincial government was established, but the government would not hear them. They wouldn't even see them. Our people were considered savages. They weren't important. Our chiefs wrote letters. I have seen a letter from a chief written around 1900 to the premier saying, "Let us talk and deal with this land question so that my grandchildren and your grandchildren can live in harmony." The "land question" still exists today.

A further intrusion was the banning of the feast. Beginning in 1884, successive versions of the Indian Act attempted to suppress the feast system. Missionaries encouraged this law because they felt it would encourage Christianization of Gitksan people. The government supported the law because officials knew people talked about "their lands."

Long ago at the feasts, we talked about our land, our ownership. It could take a year or two years for people to gather, prepare, and preserve enough to serve to all the people in the surrounding area.

They called it the big feast, the *Yukw*. It is at this feast that the official acknowledgement of a new leader is affirmed. The leader would have been "watched" for some time, perhaps a year or two. When he was deemed acceptable, the official acknowledgement was planned. All the surrounding villages were invited. It might have been a week of festivities. But, it was also very serious business. We incorporated entertainment for our guests who came to the feast. That was where land was talked about. Some of those little things are still done today, even though we don't get everything from the land. Now, we can go to the supermarket and pick up the things we need. But, in the past when they served the food the guests knew that the food came from the territory of the host of the feast.

They would lift it up before they served it. The servers would announce "This dried meat is from the host's land," and mention the name of the host of the feast. They still do that today and it's a symbol still of the people's covenant relationship to their land.

The Gitksan people never agreed to give up ownership of their territories. To this day, they have never given up the rights to their land. They felt their willingness to welcome strangers and invite others into their community was betrayed by the assumptions of newcomers to "ownership."

While our people were prepared to share the use of the land, they believed they would continue to have access themselves for berry picking and for their own fishing, hunting, and trapping needs to feed their families.

What was not clear, or was misunderstood by missionaries and government officials, was the complex structure of Gitksan society which emerged directly from the most basic of human relationships, the family. Social and economic transactions were face to face with people who knew each other very well. Exchanges were oral rather than written, and identified by both the giver and the receiver. Unethical behaviour was difficult, but if it occurred, consequences were immediate and unmistakable. Authority was based on personal respect, the integrity of the decision maker, rather than power. Political and economic decisions were by consensus, with great weight given to thoughts of those with proven ability, experience, and wisdom.

Decisions and laws were not policed. Rather, support was withdrawn from the person or group making an unpopular decision. Those offending established laws and morals lost authority in the community. Coherence was brought to the system by a constant interaction among people, often accompanied by great love. The economy extended back in time through oral histories. These histories also recorded familial ties with animals and how certain lineages came to be responsible for particular territories. The historical events recorded in story, song, and art recognized a commonality of spirit amongst humans and all living things, including land, which formed the basis of the laws governing the peoples' relationship with the rest of the world.

The feast hall was central to the political, social, spiritual, and economic life of the community:

The most important economic transactions were the sharing of wealth within the house, and reciprocated payments between houses. The reciprocity was reflected in feasts. The succession of the name and responsibilities of head chief was a central role of the feast. The feast hall gave the authority of the community to the chief and to the system as a whole. While daily interaction bound the society together, the formal exchanges at the feast reinforced the kinship structure. At a feast, a chief would accept political authority over houses other than his or her own by validating or witnessing the succession of a new head chief, by confirming the host house's territorial boundaries and river fishing sites, and by reaffirming the society's laws.

No Gitksan chief or group of chiefs had authority over all. Although each had knowledge of neighbouring houses, each chief's authority extended over a part of the society, partly overlapping that of the next chief. In this way, the whole society was woven together in a pattern reflecting kinship network.[4]

The banning of the feast hall had a profound impact on the spirituality of the people. Spirituality is the fundamental truth that sustains and gives stability to our lives. Spirituality is a profound force in our lives involving our intelligence, self-awareness, emotions, wills, and souls. Our spirituality gives us our energy.

The energy of the people, daily interactions as well as rights and responsibilities, were marked by rituals. In the feast hall, relationships were attended to. Funerals, weddings, cleansings, care of territories, and name giving were all part of the spirituality.

It is unfortunate that early missionaries did not understand and affirm the inter-relatedness of the spiritual to political, economic, and social dimensions of community life.

We harvest from the earth without disturbing or abusing it. We try to keep everything in balance. To sustain harmony with nature, our people reasoned, it was important to offer gifts in return for the gifts given us.

People attempted to direct energy in a positive way. It was considered best to do what was true, right, and good. In this way one didn't "lose energy" in covering up mistakes.

To maintain positive energy and develop spirituality, rituals were developed. Purification prepared hunters and fishermen to enter the realm of creation. Purification involved a deep concentration. It took time and energy, with the goal of the hunter to be respected by the creature who would be sacrificed for the life of the hunter and the community.

I remember a chief being arrested for holding a funeral feast. As the leader of the community, it was his social duty to ensure the carrying out of a proper funeral. When released from jail, he felt forced to have another feast, this one to cleanse his shame at being arrested. Although the law was not his own law, to be placed in jail was still a deep shame and one which required a community cleansing.

Over the years, a number of chiefs were similarly jailed. In spite of the punishments, the feasts continued to be held because of their importance to the life of the communities. We learned to use other events such as Christmas, Easter, birthdays, and Thanksgiving as occasions to serve the need to get people together and transact the business of the community. The feast didn't disappear, it went underground.

> The underground feasting helped to maintain the integrity of community relationships. However, added to the banning of the feast hall was a patriarchal social system brought by missionaries and government.

My father was designated to become chief from the time he was very young. He was head of a territory further north. When he married my mother, my mother came into that union as wealthy land-wise as my father. The term house refers to a family grouping, an extended family. Matrilineally, an extended family or house consists of a grandmother and her children, a mother and her children, and daughters and their children. Because each house owns territory, my mother came into the marriage with all the wealth of her territory, the wealth of the names we have in our clans, the songs, the history. The names were already there for the children that might come out of that union. She never changed her Gitksan name when she married my dad.

It was only after the church came in and insisted that the wives take the husband's name that chaos was created in our culture. Instead of us going with the names that my mother had, we had to take on our father's Christian name. The church taught us to take on our father's name, or because the priest had a lot of power, sometimes he would simply give names he liked to the children he baptized. My father's legal name was Clifford. That name did not reflect his connectedness to the territory, or to the house of his mother. Throughout the community, children were using names out of other houses, or names that were not connected at all with the territories.

This created great confusion for the younger people because each territory has its own group of names, and their names related to the land. The older people were flexible and they knew who people were, who their parents were, to which territory they belonged, in spite of the names they were using. The confusion arose in the minds of the younger people, because their names were no longer connected to the territories, and the responsibilities of the territories. When they were named after their father, it appeared they belonged to their father's house and territory.

Vi's family believed their children could face the changes, if they retained their self-esteem.

A Cross-Cultural Marriage

The proximity of the European and Gitksan villages meant considerable mixing between cultures, the most common being during ball games in summer and dances year-round. While Vi's family worked very hard to ensure that she had a strong sense of self, they were not quite prepared for the decisions she made and stood by:

The intrusions into the community continued in my childhood. Urged by my parents, I had an outside education, which gave me experience of the outside world. My parents also gave me another gift, the gift of self-esteem, of believing in myself. That gift of confidence enabled me to make and to stand by a decision to marry a person outside my culture.

I met my husband through community events where the cultures mixed. When we made the decision to marry, however, there were protests from both families. My husband's family, who had recently emigrated from Scotland, objected to his marrying a Native woman. My own mother vehemently objected. Future children of a union were always a consideration. My mother wanted our children to have the benefit of both a mother's and father's houses and inheritance. She said any children would have no identity in the community. My father suggested adopting my husband into his house and clan. In this way, my children had identity and inheritance through my mother's house, the Fireweed clan, as well as through their father's adopted clan, the Frog clan.

It is ironic that the strength of her self-esteem and culture made it possible for Vi to marry outside her culture. Her family responded to her decision with new growth and adaptations of traditional understandings to incorporate the new family member. Vi's husband had grown up in the town of New Hazelton, where his father was employed by the railway.

Vi married John Smith, nicknamed Scotty, in a house wedding. They were married by an Anglican priest and remained married for 52 years.

Although she continued to be recognized as a chief's daughter, with all the rights and privileges of the position within her own community, at her marriage, Canadian law took away her Gitksan status. Vi's children also lost their legal status as full members of the Gitksan community.

In the early years of marriage, I was very busy with the children. My first commitment was to my family. My husband worked long hours supporting the family with his trucking business. I was helped by my mother, who grew a large garden and shared her abundant harvests with me and my young family. Our first home was rented. Then, in 1945 we built a home very near the centre of the village of Hazelton on a lot purchased from the town.

It was hard to do all the housekeeping and look after all the children. I often hired young women from the village to help with the housework. Even so, I often found myself up until one and two in the morning ironing or cleaning. It was the only way I found to keep up with the housework and care of the children.

I loved gardening and grew a large raspberry patch. I liked the children to play in the yard, so didn't trouble myself with keeping the lawn overly tidy until they were grown. I enjoyed cooking. I've baked bread for the family all my life, and I still do, at times. The grandchildren love it.

The birth of our youngest daughter was a great delight to the elders of Kispiox village. My mother had died a few years earlier. On the birth of my daughter, the elders came to the hospital to see her, bringing gifts for a girl. When I wondered how they could possibly know the baby was a girl, they explained that my mother had come to them in a dream and had told them she was coming back and would live with me! I could believe that because she had always said that she would like to have light hair. I wonder now whether she experienced racism. Her appearance was very Gitksan. She had long black hair, very straight, and dark eyes. She used to say she'd like to be blond with curly hair, and blue eyes. Our youngest daughter is the only one with light hair.

Our daughter was at times distraught by the great attention and affection she received from those elders, and by the fact that they called her by her my mother's name. I explained to her when she grew older why they treated her as they did. They really believed her spirit was her grandmother's. When she met and married a young man from Kispiox and went there to live, the elders were really happy. They felt she was returning to Kispiox where she belonged.

One of the gifts of our culture is that we believe the ancestors are there to guide us. They have set a road for us, and they're still there, still guiding us.

> Scotty was popular with all the villagers. Children of the village knew he kept candy and gum in his pockets at all times, and they always scrambled after him for treats. He loved all animals and kept dog biscuits in his truck. When he was visiting his friends, he brought treats for their pets.
>
> He was friendly and comfortable with both cultures, accepting of cultural values of the Gitksan, and known by many, in part because of his trucking business. He worked long hours, and very hard. Although adopted into the Frog clan, Scotty never attended feasts or ceremonies.
>
> Over a space of 18 years, Vi gave birth to 10 children—seven boys and three girls. One of the boys died tragically at the age of two.

When the children were young, I didn't feel able to attend the feasts. They often lasted until the early hours of the morning and I didn't feel able to stay out late and still care for young children. I did carry out my obligations as a member of my mother's house to offer gifts and help with food at feasts. This was quite a commitment because I was always in a position of giving, without ever being in a position to "receive back" the gifts of others.

The ban on the feast hall was lifted shortly after Vi was married. Although unable to be involved in the activities of the feast hall because of the needs of her own young family, Vi was as supportive as she was able to be.

Spirituality and the Anglican church was very important to Vi. Scotty encouraged her to continue to attend it and take the children to Sunday school there rather than to the church of his childhood. Throughout the years she faithfully attended St. Peter's, involved as a teacher, lay reader, with women's work, and serving at several Synods. Her commitment to the church didn't go unnoticed.

As the children grew, I began to be more involved in the cultural activities of my community. When my mother died, there was a real change in the direction of my life. I was asked by house elders to take on the name of my grandmother, the name Wii Bistaii. This I accepted under protest, as I knew the heavy responsibility carried with the name.

The elders believed that in her life she would heal and touch people. Over the next 30 years, they continually reached out to teach and guide her. Wii Bistaii means 'great grouse,' and refers to the legend of the great drumming grouse who gave its life so the ancestors of the Gitksan could be saved from starvation. The name is given in trust only to those who are believed capable spiritually of making sacrifices necessary to guide with wisdom.

A Healing Vision

Over the years, Vi had been witnessing the impact of over 50 years of laws against the practice of cultural traditions. The impact was felt in every family. Vi and Scotty lived close to the middle of Hazelton. Often when she looked out her window, she saw tiny children going to school, their hair uncombed, their clothing unkempt. She wanted to bring them in and hug them, care for them, comb their hair.

The centrality of the family, and the complex kinship structure, had been immediately affected by the influx of the newcomers, although in the first generation of contact, the impact was more easily absorbed because newcomers were transient, mostly traders who came and left, as her own grandfather had done.

The community had dealt with the earliest newcomers with allowances for differences, caring for children of these unions within house and clan. Relationships were formalized in the feast hall. The termination of a relationship was also recognized in the feast hall. Changing relationships were part of community life. The birth of a child was always welcomed. The special place of children was rooted in ancestral story and tradition.

An attitude of acceptance applied to a woman having a child outside of marriage as defined by missionaries. Gitksan believed that the child was always legitimate. A child was never what the larger society viewed as "illegitimate," because a child always has at least one parent, and this was the mother. In fact, in a small community, except in very unusual circumstances, the identity of the father is usually known. In an era when the missionaries came, people began to frown on single mothers. But this is changing back again to the acceptance which has always been present in our own culture, an acceptance rooted in story.

Long ago, after the flood, there were two sisters out on the territories. There were some things the sisters found difficult to do, and because of this, a man was sent to help them. It turned out that he was an angel. A sexual relationship developed with this angel and one of the sisters. She became pregnant, and when the two sisters returned to the village, they had a small baby. They named the baby with a word which in our language means 'it was lost, I found it.'

However, the imposition of a patrilineal social structure and Canadian law meant that the knowledge that each child should have a place in community, should be cared for, was no longer in place.

Within a few generations, the social disintegration had so increased that only a few elders knew and understood Gitksan values. They tried to carry on with their values of hard work and sharing with others less fortunate. They transferred their skills to modern technology, often having three freezers in their homes, one for themselves, one for children and grandchildren, and one for those in need.

Those in need soon outnumbered those able to help. Children especially needed to understand the strong positive cultural values of the community, and to have a sense of pride in identity. Vi felt deeply the pain of children not knowing their identities, and mistreatment and abuses they suffered.

The decision to accept the healing name of her grandmother, Wii Bistaii, had been rooted in her leadership that had included involvement in the church from her earliest years as well as involvement in her house. More and more people were aware of the despair of children. Many were being abused. Many responded in self-destructive ways, through abuse of alcohol and in suicide. She was asked to give workshops, to try to help leaders welcome children. She did so by encouraging integrations of Gitksan and Christian understandings:

There are many similarities between the Christian and the traditional ways of the Gitksan peoples. It is important to understand our own Gitksan ways, and it is important to understand the Christian. We must each take responsibility to learn more of the "Good News" in order to teach the younger generation. One cannot teach what one doesn't have.

Above everything else we do, we need to love the children, to establish a relationship and show a real interest in each child. Children need to know we are interested in their well-being.

We need to pray sincerely for our children, and to seek the Holy Spirit. We need to share in love to others, remembering that we need to love ourselves before we are able to love others. We need to talk about true forgiveness, and unconditional love.

We are called "Children of God," and it is wonderful. Children belong in the family, and our relationship to God is therefore a given. We are not alien beings attempting to create a relationship with a distant and indifferent Creator, but children of a God who cares. Children can expect to be protected. God is active and lives in our world, defending, guarding, nourishing, and guiding us.

Children are not asked to be sophisticated, but to follow a few simple guidelines, constantly expected to love and to follow. We, as children, need role models. Parents and teachers know that the best way to teach our children is to get down beside them, at their level, and give them example. A big person standing up or behind a desk can be intimidating to a small child. Lectures and thick manuals or preaching about their mistakes are not helpful. A parent or teacher sitting on the floor saying, “Let me show you how,” is always the better way.

We teach them to love one another. Love is the opposite of hate and murder. Love gives life. One cannot love God and hate others. Love is expressive, not possessive. One cannot love God and fail to share what one has with others.

We are told to bear one another’s burdens. Since the power comes from God, and the strength God gives us to love is limitless, we have no need or reason to keep it to ourselves. It was given to us to share, not to keep. Sharing God’s gifts is another way to experience freedom. It is all too easy to think of gifts in terms of possessions, things like bank accounts, and heirloom china, or jewellery that we have to protect and worry about. How can I really be free if I have to worry about holding the fort, protecting my possessions? But the gifts God gives us are free and need no protecting. How can anyone steal a gift I’m trying to give others?

Paul says, “Let’s have no conceit or envy.” If someone else has greater gifts, praise God! All God’s gifts are for sharing and strengthening the church. Bear one another’s burdens is the Christian way. This is another way of understanding freedom. If your burden is too heavy, put it down and take on someone else’s. It appears that those who are willing to help others are most likely to be offered help themselves. Paul is pointing us towards a path of love without limit, the Spirit to strengthen us, the sharing of burdens being the way to freedom.

In the twelfth chapter of Hebrews Jesus has given us both an example and all the evidence we need of the victory God has promised to those who are faithful. We are not only asked to witness, but to remember that we are also being witnessed. “Clouds of witnesses surround us.” Our progress is watched. They pray for us.

To remind us what our faith is, we should consider Paul’s letter to Hebrews, chapter 11. This marvellous catalogue is of those who bore witness in the past, who sought for something more than this world can give. This cloud of witness makes a difference. At times, we feel alone and abandoned. As Christians, we shouldn't feel this way. Through Christ we are linked with others who have made their witness a long time ago. They observe our struggle. Think of our grandparents, our parents, and members of our extended family. We are strengthened and supported by the depth of their love and concern. It makes a difference. It is comforting to know that we are not alone.

Galatians 6 says "A new Creation is everything." This is our bottom line. Not law, but a new Creation. Words like freedom, Spirit, and love help us to understand this new Creation. These are words that work from within to inspire us, as compared to words that work from outside to compel. Paul is describing a radical re-orientation of the way human society has always worked, and still does. We, who call ourselves Christian, are still the revolutionaries who imagine a world in which true freedom is still possible and love is the prime motive and the Spirit guides our lives. Even within the church we lack the courage to commit ourselves fully to such a world.

But, we glimpse it. Sometimes we glimpse it in an elderly shut-in who has only love to share, sometimes in a child who takes the gospel seriously and expects us to be role models, sometimes in a congregation which makes a difference in a community. This glimpse is the new Creation. That glimpse is important.

We will be judged by our actions, not our words. If we disagree, we do it gently. We try not to create divisions. Here are some wonderful words to put into practice: "Pursue righteousness, faith, love, and peace...[the Lord's servant must...be... kindly to everyone, an] apt teacher, patient, correcting opponents with gentleness" [2 Timothy 2:22, 24 , 25]. Our faith is not built on words. We have a firm foundation in the fact that the Lord knows those who are his [John 10:14]. It is God's church, not ours. We must trust God to protect it.

As we consider the future, we have to be critical as well. The church has to change, or it's going to die. Perhaps it is right for the present form of the church to die, so that a new form may surface which will better serve the purpose. The question we need to ask is: will we be strong enough to allow what's not working to die? We have to think about our children.[5]

Vi's commitment to the future of children called her to action. She worked more and more intentionally on cultural recovery. A recognized elder now, she was one of the few who continued to speak and understand her language. Gitksan cultural understandings are rooted within the Gitksan language, with meaning behind every word. The storytelling and song sharing were critical in making connections:

Songs have importance in Gitksan life, being composed to mark important historic events and carried and owned in a family and house to be used at special occasions. Similarly oral histories have special importance. They were important in ancient times, but they have significance now because they are living in connections between the past and the present.

She began to share stories in schools to help children understand their cultural past. She encouraged the remembering of old songs and the composition of new songs. As she was working quietly in church and community to encourage recovery of culture, a crisis of momentous proportions occurred.

By the early 1980s clearcutting by large companies began without the consent of the people. Early logging procedures had been similar to the harvesting procedures of the Gitksan. Small sawmills, some owned by local Gitksan peoples, contributed to the local economy, and were seen by many as an acceptable part of the development of the area, bringing cash to supplement the people's incomes. Even in the early years, however, there had been tension between the forestry industry and the Gitksan peoples because land claims hadn't been settled. When clearcutting began, the hearts of the people were torn. It hurt them psychologically to see their lands so devastated, rich forests for which they had cared for generations were left completely barren, desolate.

The conflict her ancestors had warned about a century before now escalated. Married to a man involved indirectly in the forestry industry through trucking, Vi was acutely aware of how much people in the community needed job opportunities provided by forestry. While she felt free to express her thoughts to her husband within their marriage, she also respected his beliefs and supported him. Increasing tensions within the village saddened her. Her own children experienced the conflicts deeply, as some were married within the Gitksan community and others were married to Europeans.

Younger members of the community approached her:

I was asked to participate in a research project to assist with land claims. They were preparing for negotiations in my community. At first, I thought, no! My husband is retiring soon, and I can't do it. I was adamant that I didn't want to get involved, in spite of my belief that the land claims process was right for Gitksan people. I was really living in two cultures, and I felt I knew how most of the white community felt. It was difficult because I was married to someone in the white community, and many white people, many people I knew, were against the claims. While I adamantly said "No!", I was thinking about it.

The young men gave Vi a week to think this through. She struggled with the decision. Then, like the prophets of old, she was moved to action:

One night in the middle of the night, I just woke up, and decided, I have to do this. It seemed right.

To prepare for the work, a group of Gitksans went to Ottawa to study at Carleton University for several months under the director of a program for historical research. Their training prepared them for research work which deepened our understanding and knowledge of the oral literary traditions of my culture. For five years, I was involved in a meticulous research process in which we recorded on tape the stories, legends, and knowledge of elders. These recordings were then transcribed and used in a land claims process by the Gitksan and Wet'suwet'en chiefs.

In October 1984 Gitksan and Wet'suwet'en chiefs filed a statement of claims against the provincial government, seeking a declaration that they have a right to ownership of, and jurisdiction over, their House Territories. The actual court case was *Delgam Uukwx vs. the Crown, Her Majesty the Queen*. It began in 1987 in the town of Smithers, 50 miles [80 kilometres] east of Hazelton. The court case was expected to last up to six months. In fact, it lasted three years. It was moved to Vancouver because the judge was close to retirement, and found the travel to be too exhausting. Our elders were not considered. We had to fly our elders to Vancouver to participate in the case. We accommodated the judge at the expense of our own elders.

Canadian courts do not accept accounts from an oral literary tradition. Therefore, the Gitksan peoples prepared for the court process by transcribing the oral accounts of elders.

The court process brought out the differences in values between Gitksan peoples and the Canadian court of law. While the judge wore a robe, Gitksan chiefs and elders were not permitted to. It was hard dealing with the viciousness of the court process. But, there was growth and learning. For my part, I understood that the viciousness was associated with each side attempting to best defend the interests of its clients. The interpreters were often in a position of receiving the anger of the defence counsels acting on behalf of the provincial and federal governments.

Although I found this difficult, I felt it preferable to the elders receiving the anger. The trial, which went on into the spring of 1990, ended with a ruling against the Gitksan and Wet'suwet'en peoples. [In June of 1997, their case was presented to the Supreme Court of Canada.] This was a great disappointment for the people. It was terrible when the verdict was announced. No one said anything for a long time. We just couldn't believe it. You want to believe in justice, that the right thing will be done, but sometimes it seems it will not happen in our lifetime. Perhaps it will happen in the lives of our children and grandchildren.

For Vi, the experience of doing research was fascinating. She found she knew all the words, although she often didn't know why certain words were used in certain contexts. In her research, Vi has often felt the stories of elders should be written down. As she says, there is much to be done in sharing the knowledge that elders hold.

There is a difficulty, however, in that one doesn't always know where others are in their understandings. She had people say to her: "Why didn't you tell me this 10 or 15 years ago?" Her response is often: "I was ready to tell; you weren't ready to listen."

Vi and many other elders are increasingly aware that there are fewer people who know and understand the language and are able to carry the teachings. In a few years, when the people are prepared to listen, it will be important for the information to be available, either on tape or in publications. For this reason, she feels compelled to describe the stories of Gitksan people, and their place in Gitksan society.

Her husband encouraged her to remain involved in the cultural life of her community, which included research into land claims, and in the same way had encouraged her to attend the Anglican church early in their life together. He knew this was important to her. She describes their last few years together as very rich, very good. Knowing that he was terminally ill, they discussed and worked out many things they had been unable to come to terms with earlier.

At times, the antagonism and hostility towards Vi when she was involved in research in the land claims process were so great that she found it difficult to continue the workshop process locally. There were times when the surrounding communities would invite workshops. When they saw an elder woman arrive, they were often angry. Vi believed they were angry because they expected to have a young man to argue with. In their anger, they sometimes treated her with great disrespect, something she never experienced in her own community.

This was at first a shock to her, but caused her to be even more aware of the differences between cultures. Within her own community, disrespect of an elder would not be tolerated. There, her eldership had been increasingly affirmed, and her early commitment to the church has continued.

A Weaver of Story

The small huts with family relics once prevalent in the graveyards have been vandalized and burned. The church that used to remain open and welcoming is now locked when not in use because of similar vandalism.

Over the years Vi has never felt disregarded or unaffirmed as a Native person within her own small parish. She has served as a lay reader, often filling in for the priest when he or she was away or on vacation.

She has sometimes felt resentment of non-Native attitudes—but throughout has never lost her faith in God, with the creation of all that is wonderful and necessary for survival. Over time, she has come to accept trials and skepticism as part of her spiritual growth.

The colonization process left First Nations people with a low self-esteem. Vi's recent experience is that the church is opening doors. A part of her desire is for First Nations peoples to help to open the door a bit wider, enabling the church to get to know all First Nations peoples better.

In Vi's words, "This is the way to forgiveness and healing." She believes that the church will continue to support First Nations' struggles for freedom from oppression. She was particularly moved by the support from the Anglican and United churches in their land claim.

With understandings of the importance of story, Vi weaves her vision for the future, a vision for a church and a society where women, men, children, and nature will be given their rightful places of acceptance, honour, and respect:

I see a universe. It is a huge view. Studying the blackness, millions of separate, growing worlds are hanging, poised. Each world suspended there in the dark emptiness has a name, an identity. All the worlds have moons, some many, some few, spinning brightly around in their orbits. Yes, there are many worlds, but they are very small. One person, one animal, or one plant sits precariously on each one. Reaching out from my world I can almost grasp my moons, almost, and I see surrounding me, enticing me, all the other worlds in endless beautiful array, separate, alone. I cannot reach them.

Is this truly a vision of our planet? Are we one world or many? If we are many, how can we contact the worlds that surround us? If we are one, why do we so blatantly ignore our connections? In these days seared by war, ravaged by disease, abuse, environmental crises, to speak of weaving our worlds seems almost a cruel joke.

A flock of birds, one unit is composed of many identities. Each part is beautiful, functional, distinctive. Together they inspire and uplift. Our spirits rise with their rising. Weaving our worlds, perhaps we could reach if we touched the threads that make the melding. I believe in connections. Consider "what if" for a moment, to catch this concept. How much different would life be in this community if the moment of our conception had been delayed? You would not be here. What would that mean?

Think of your families, your friends, your colleagues at work. You touch many people. None of these contacts would exist if you didn't. Think of the future, how different it might be. The significance of your non-being is profound.

All of this is simply musing. We cannot change the past or know the future. Yet we can learn from this musing. Each action and moment in history determines many other moments. The alteration of one thing, however small it appears, does not stand alone. Instead, it connects one thing to another in labyrinthine patterns. Everything in the universe is threaded together. We need to know this as we know our own name, for it is just as much an aspect of our identity.

We are each separate and unique, but we are also related to each other. There is great value in our individuality, but individuality only has real meaning within the context of interdependence.

The sun on a bird's wing, a raindrop pulled through the soil to the roots of a plant, and rocks falling unseen, unheard in the mountains are events which weave tiny momentous changes in the unfolding design.

If you cry, it changes the pattern. I may not know how it alters things for me. I may not ever know you wept or why. But it matters still, for we are connected, you and I. It is the way of all life.

What does all this mean on a practical level? It means that any war will have repercussions the world over. It means that how I respond to those repercussions makes a difference to the present movement towards peace.

It means that the fact that people in our community were taken from their families and sent to residential schools years ago alters life here now for all of us.

It means that the way we harvest our forests has an impact on everyone. It is not idle to say that the destruction of the rain forests has global implications. We impact the environment. We affect one another.

The extinction of a single species will rearrange our future and many disappear each day. If other species are in danger—so are we. Every living thing is important because it is unique and because it is a part of creation, a part of the whole. Each life is valuable, a distinct individual, a thread in the total fibre.

Connections are threads of existence. One could create an entire warping and weft together to create an open webbing, choosing a large range of colours and textures. The threads could represent the earth, the sky, the water, and everything alive which dances its life out on this planet. The many colours of every earth and animal species, the races of our own human species are indicated within the context of the whole. All mesh to create unity, not one string is unaffected by another. The weaver doesn't know when beginning how each thread of this woven structure influences the final piece. That it does influence the final piece is inevitable. Within the lattice work of essential connections, all manner of intricate weaving can take place with a whole variety of threads.

It is at this moment that we must consider, that we must take up our tools to weave within the weaving.

In the church, we come together men and women of all ages, of different backgrounds. We come as children whose vision of the world is yet uncluttered and as older people whose years provide a special kind of insight. Our cultures differ. Our personalities, our spiritual understanding, our education, heartaches, and joys are all different.

The differences are important because the connections are in reality so powerful. These differences, like the colours and textures of the weaving, make our work beautiful. All our differences make the weaving more beautiful. Where we really meet is in the heart. Being open in this way, in our heart, is a web that makes our weaving strong. How could we do without either our differences, or our meeting in the heart?

We wish to weave within the structure of our unity the beauty of all that is unique in each of us. How do we do this? What are our tools?

We begin with language. Sometimes in the history of people, the use of gesture could no longer contain the ideas emerging within individuals and in the context of developing cultures. Language came out of cultures expressing in a particular way the concepts encountered as each group of people made contact with their surroundings in their own special way. That it is translatable is the statement of our unity. That each language is different is a statement of how much we have to offer one another.

The Chinese language has retained through centuries the pictorial nature of its expression. The picture word itself embodies the meaning, describes the concept presented. Three characters, for instance create the word LOVE. The first character is receive, the second heart, the third friend. To LOVE becomes—to receive the heart of a friend. When Chinese people say the word

LOVE, all that surrounds these three characters goes with the speaking.[6]

In my own language, Gitksan, many words are built around the word heart (*goot*). *Lu aamhl goodee*, 'I am glad,' literally means 'my heart is happy.' *Luusa halxus goodee*, 'I am astonished' or 'I am awed,' literally means 'my heart is going up.'

This is not sentimentality. The people who long ago invented these words recognized the emotional centre of many experiences, acknowledged this and celebrate it in their language.

This provides a lesson for us. The phrase for unity, for instance, *lungxii goadem*, means 'we are of one heart.' In English, we speak of unity also. The English word means oneness as well, but it does not convey the source of unity, the meeting of hearts....

Within the body of the church there are many cultures, many languages. My knowledge is limited, but I am confident that every language our species has devised is equally rich.

We also have the capacity to enter the world of others. We need to do this. When we see someone in sorrow we want to put our arms around that person—to say without words "I feel your sorrow too." Touching can indicate acceptance, caring. We may touch with our hands, our eyes. We may touch at a level which acknowledges the value of another person, and open the door to both vulnerability and trust. Dangerous ground!

There are some people I meet whom I discover I do not like. This doesn't happen often, but it does happen. Perhaps you experience the same now and then. Occasionally circumstances result in close contact with someone I don't like. Their manner, their attitudes, their ideology, their arrogance may put me off. Yet, I may be stuck with the contact, forced into relationship by circumstance.

We need languages as a prime tool in communication. If our language is impoverished, so are we, and our ability to weave is reduced. Language emerges from cultures providing a way to communicate the threads which unite us and those which reflect our diversity. With language we may come out of ourselves. We are able to express ideas, share what is separate and what is common, give voice to hope and despair, or ask for help and give support. With language we reach outward. Our voices make it possible for us to be received.

We must take care not to belittle any languages or the cultures which brought them to birth. If one language is good it does not follow that others are not. Let us share our own heritage and allow others to enrich us with theirs. Let us receive the heart of a friend.

Intimacy itself is a tool for weaving. Good weaving requires familiarity with our materials. We are the woven and the weavers. We are the materials, touching, coming in contact with, knowing one another. Our language can facilitate this, but alone it is not enough. You may speak, but will I listen? And if I listen, will I care to understand? The other side of voice is silence: open receptive silence.

Over time as I become familiar with another person, I learn to see underneath. Intimacy forces me to re-evaluate my judgements. Significant contact always changes people. Still, the things that may have bothered me about another person and those things in me which bothered that person may not have disappeared at all. What has changed is our viewpoint. We have touched one another. We know each other in a new way. This "knowing" makes it possible to love. Some of the people I have met with initial distaste are now among my closest friends. We are not more "compatible" with one another than we ever were, yet we have come together.

Truly it is not easy to know anyone, even those we like. All the things which can enrich us also serve to push us apart—our cultures, religions, colours, our varied personalities and interests. No one agrees on everything or experiences the world the same way. When we face differences our only hope is to turn to open-receptive silence. We must really hear. We must listen with intent to understand. Such weaving is most difficult and complex. It is intricate, "touching souls" makes it possible.

The resultant whole weaving shows artistic integrity of a superior nature. This takes time and is a deeply moving work. It is born in the inter-texture of diverse identities. In this weaving, those who are different acknowledge one another with respect. It's okay to be different. Open silence, listening to really hear, leads to deep touching of spirits. This is an essential tool in our weaving.

Traditionally, in cultures all over the world, women have woven. They are makers of clothing, woven containers like baskets for so many uses, for shelter and objects of beauty to open our hearts to joy. Weaving gives comfort, service, protection, and pleasure—and pleasure is important to affirm. Weaving takes time. It is painstaking, and even tedious.

For centuries women have watched children, moment by moment, day by day, year by year, grow from tiny helpless bundles to strong adults with vision and purpose. Women know it takes time to achieve things of value. The world and we within it feel a searching pain these days. We want to hurry. It is an instant society. So much seems so urgent, and it is! But, we can't afford to rush. Now, more than ever we must trust our sense of time to build values that last. We need to weave well.

Patience is another tool in this weaving we do. Our societies emphasize the importance of intelligence and education. Logical thinking is given great respect. To have our power of reason is considered a noble goal. The human intellect is of considerable value. But many women, I believe, realize at an intuitive level that this is not enough.

There are connections between us that are separate from all reasonable thinking. There are resources which work from within and beyond, then shine forth from some people. We recognize in them something different from fine intelligence. We recognize wisdom and real humility. We need not look for people of wisdom and humility in high places. They are all around us. The resources of the Spirit are accessible to all. We have the capacity to acknowledge and draw from a power beyond our own limitations.

I speak softly about spirituality. In our understanding of spirituality, we touch on hope, conviction, mystery, and God. These understandings are extremely personal. Yet, these are central values of our being which unify the others, providing courage and strength to continue to weave, to use our tools to enrich the whole when it feels impossible to do so.

I need to introduce one more word, one more concept. That word is crisis. We live in a world in "crisis." Chinese people describe this word using two characters. The first means opportunity, the second, danger.

This pictorial description illuminates two things. First, we tend to hear the word crisis and throw up our hands in despair. Crisis to us often implies the end of it all. We feel in danger, alone. We are in fear. Let's consider the balance the Chinese people give us. With their understanding, we receive freedom to hope. Crisis is not hopeless. In crisis there is choice, and in this choice lies the second insight. There is choice, but our Canadian culture is not a balanced one at present. We tend to swing one way, then another. We must try to recognize the hope in the midst of crisis, but we cannot forget the danger either.

War continues to tear our world. Our planet is threatened by human carelessness and self-centred greed. Our children are abused. Neither women or men understand their value or their beauty. Crisis does not come upon us bestowing good or evil willy-nilly. Crisis involves choices, and these choices are our choices, our responsibility.

We can turn our weaving tools to good use or to poor use. We may disregard or we may respect. We may fear or we may love. To respect and love takes a good deal of work. To disregard or avoid because of fear is much easier at first. The resultant devastation, however, is tremendous. We cannot possibly measure the cost! We have a crisis. We have choices. We have a responsibility to make changes.

War makes a difference. It alters the web of this planet. The tree that falls in the forest makes a difference. The fish that dies in the waters makes a difference. Each part of this weaving, however large or small, alters the rest.

The open arms of Mother Teresa make a difference. The loving L'Arche communities make a difference. The soup kitchens make a difference. Women's shelters, halfway houses, and children's help lines make a difference. The doctor and nurse's gentle hands and voice as they comfort a patient dying of cancer or AIDS make a difference. Youth in our communities who volunteer in hospitals or playgrounds make a difference. A mother or father's arms around a little son or daughter as she or he rocks the child to sleep. These are all part of the weaving, and our small acts of kindness, these choices affect the weaving.

I passionately believe we are connected. Therefore, I must believe also that I matter. The small moments in my life have significance. What I do in a tiny way makes a difference. What you do makes a difference.

We cannot say some words of power that will suddenly end human greed and bring peace and justice to the world. What can we do? We are individuals. Those of us who are women have been called weavers, nurturers. Are these roles thrust upon us, roles that we must in principle resist? Or will we choose to weave, to nurture, as women free to choose? Will men more and more affirm the nurturing in their own persons?

What will it mean if each of us make this choice, in our families, in our schools, our churches, our communities?
What if we choose to respect the person next door who drinks too much alcohol? What if we give the woman just out of jail a job? What if we teach our children that colour and culture are like beautiful "packages"? Each person of every culture and colour enriches the world, and each person has a soul very much like ours. What if we ask an elder for support, for courage and advice? Are we able to trust their experience in troubled times or times of joy? What might happen if we ask to learn a language that is not our own or explore another culture? What are the possibilities if we face our child—gently and in humility—when anger has controlled our judgement and say "I am sorry"? Are we able to say, "I was wrong, I treated you wrongly. I ask your forgiveness"?

We can do these things—and so much more. This is possible for all of us. These things are not exclusive to women, nor should they be, but it might be easier for us because we have traditionally been "weavers," nurturers. If we, as women, weave well, the next generation of women and men might not be as restricted as ours.

Choose what is important to you and work your piece of the whole weaving. Perhaps there are issues that touch your heart—the uplifting of human value, a concern to defuse violence, care of the environment, racism, or land claims. Perhaps you'll be less active in what seems to be larger issues and will recognize your strength in your job, your home, or your school, in bringing laughter or giving song.

Wherever you have influence, wherever you find your skills, wherever you have a sense of purpose—this is where you should weave. Give yourself to it. Believe in its value, its beauty, its necessity.

Alone we weave, together we weave. Let's choose our patterns and make them lovely, because each one of us makes a difference.[7]

Vi now lives in a small bungalow in Gitanmaax. Her living room window looks out over Stekyoodinahl, and mists rise from the valley below. Her kettle is frequently "on," and her phone rings often. Children, grandchildren, family, and friends continue to seek her advice. She continues to bake bread, to the delight of her grandchildren.

She encourages young women and men alike to aim for an excellent education. She encourages bridging of spiritualities, having raised her own children to respect the culture of their father, as well as her own Gitksan culture. Four of Vi's children remain in the local community. One lives in the nearby town of Smithers, and two live in the city of Prince George. The other two live in Abbotsford and Kamloops. Some have chosen to continue to practise Gitksan cultural traditions.

This collection of Vi's writings, edited from talks and workshops across Canada, reflects that the trust of the elders in her healing gifts was well placed. In her lifetime, Wii Bistaii has become an extraordinary healer, building deep and firm bridges between spiritualities of the Gitksan and the many people who have come to call this country their home.

She seeks to make the world a better place for all our children and grandchildren.

Appendix One
Apologies to Native People

In 1986, an apology was presented to Native people by the Moderator of The United Church of Canada at General Council in Sudbury, Ontario.

> Long before my people journeyed to this land, your people were here, and you received from your elders an understanding of creation, and of the mystery that surrounds us all that was deep and rich and to be treasured. We did not hear you when you shared your vision. In our zeal to tell you of the good news of Jesus Christ we were closed to the value of your spirituality. We confused western ways and culture with the depth and breadth and length and height of the gospel of Christ. We imposed our civilization as a condition of accepting the gospel. We tried to make you be like us and in so doing we helped to destroy the vision that made you what you were. As a result you, and we, are poorer and the image of the Creator in us is twisted, blurred and we are not what we are meant by God to be. We ask you to forgive us and to walk together with us in the spirit of Christ so that our peoples may be blessed and God's creation healed.

In 1993, in Minaki, Ontario, the Primate of the Anglican Church of Canada delivered an apology:

> A Message from the Primate of the Anglican Church of Canada
> Minaki,Ontario,
> Friday, August 6, 1993
>
> My Brothers and Sisters:
>
> Together here with you I have listened as you have told your stories of the residential schools. I have heard

the voices that have spoken of pain and hurt experienced in the schools, and of the scars which endure to this day.

I have felt shame and humiliation as I have heard of suffering inflicted by my people and as I think of the part our church played in that suffering.

I am deeply conscious of the sacredness of the stories that you have told, and I hold in the highest honour those who have told them.

I have heard with admiration the stories of people and communities who have worked at healing, and I am aware of how much more healing is needed.

I also know that I am in need of healing, and my own people are in need of healing, and our church is in need of healing. Without that healing we will continue the same attitudes that have done such damage in the past.

I know that healing takes a long time, both for people and for communities.

I also know that it is God who heals and that God can begin to heal when we open ourselves, our wounds, our failure, and our shame, to God. I want to take one step along that path here and now.

I accept and I confess, before God and you, our failures in the residential schools. We failed you. We failed ourselves. We failed God.

I am sorry, more than I can say, that we were a part of a system which took you and your children from home and family.

I am sorry, more than I can say, that we tried to remake you in our image, taking from you your language and the signs of your identity.

I am sorry, more than I can say, that in our schools so many were abused physically, sexually, culturally, and emotionally.

On behalf of the Anglican Church of Canada, I present our apology.

I do this at the desire of those in the Church, like the National Executive Council, who know some of your stories and have asked me to apologize.

I do this in the name of many who do not know these stories.

And I do this even though there are those in the church who cannot accept the fact that these things were done in our name.

As soon as I am home, I shall tell all the bishops what I have said, and ask them to co-operate with me and with the National Executive Council in helping this healing at the local level. Some bishops have already begun this work.

I know how often you have heard words which have been empty because they have not been accompanied by actions. I pledge to you my best efforts, and the efforts of our church at the national level, to walk with you along the path of God's healing.

The work of the Residential Schools Working Group, the video, the commitment and the effort of the Special Assistants to the Primate for this work, and the grants available for the healing conferences are some signs of that pledge; and we shall work for others.

This is Friday, the day of Jesus' suffering and death. It is the anniversary of the first atomic bomb at Hiroshima, one of the most terrible injuries ever inflicted by one people on another.

But even atomic bombs and Good Friday are not the last word. God raised Jesus from the dead as a sign that life and wholeness are the everlasting and unquenchable purpose of God.

Thank you for listening to me

Archbishop and Primate

Appendix Two
The Impact of Residential Schools

This material has been adapted from the Royal Commission on Aboriginal People: A Special Consultation with Historic Mission Churches, prepared by Terry Thompson and John Bird in 1993 for the Anglican Church of Canada. The history of the United Church residential schools is similar and may be obtained through the Royal Commission on Aboriginal Peoples.

The Early Mission Period

The relationship between First Nations and the Anglican Church began in 1753 in Atlantic Canada with the appointment of the Reverend Thomas Wood as missionary to the Micmac people. He was sponsored by the Society for the Propagation of the Gospel (SPG), an independent church missionary society in Britain. Other initiatives followed. In 1786 the New England Company began to employ Anglican Mission agents in New Brunswick. In Upper Canada the first Aboriginal Anglicans were Loyalists who arrived as refugees from the American War of Independence. Anglican Mohawks established settlements on the Bay of Quinte and at Brantford, where they built the first Protestant church. Aboriginal lay readers provided regular Sunday services which were supplemented by semi-annual visits from clergy.

The first generation of missionary effort produced Native Christians who became missionaries to their own people.

A Shift in Focus

A major change in missionary policy in the mid-nineteenth century was the move to establish residential schools. This was partly the result of a perception among mission workers that it was more productive to focus on converting Aboriginal children than to try to convert the adults. This change had a profound effect on Aboriginal people as it reduced their input into the missionary project and discouraged the further development of Indigenous Anglican leadership.

Residential schools established in the mid-nineteenth century reflected a government policy of assimilation of Native people. The first residential school had been established by John West in the Red River area of Manitoba, near present day Winnipeg, in 1820. He wrote in his diary:

> I had to establish the principle that the North American Indian of these regions would part from his children, to be educated in the white man's knowledge and religion.

Some Aboriginal leaders, recognizing the need for their children to become familiar with the settlers' language and culture, and wanting them to have a Christian education, had encouraged the establishment of residential schools. More commonly, the schools were imposed and had the effect of cutting Native children off from their own cultures, languages and lifestyles.

More information on the history of residential schools and the impact of these schools of First Nations is available through Anglican Book Centre and The United Church of Canada.

PRINT RESOURCES

Breaking the Silence: An Interpretive Study of Residential School Impact and Healing as Illustrated by the Stories of First Nations Individuals. Ottawa: Assembly of First Nations, 1994.

Carlson, Joyce, editor. *Dancing the Dream: The First Nations and the Church in Partnership.*Toronto: Anglican Book Centre, 1995. First Nations people tell their stories and reflect on their spirituality in relation to the church. Includes residential school stories from the 1993 First Nations Convocation at Minaki Lodge, Kenora, Ontario.

Engelstadt, Diane and John Bird, editors. *Nation to Nation: Aboriginal Sovereignty and the Future of Canada*. Concord, Ontario: Anansi Press, 1992.

Royal Commission on Aboriginal Peoples: Special Consultation with the Historic Mission Churches. Nov. 8–9, 1993. A report containing briefs from the Anglican Church of Canada, the Canadian Conference of Catholic Bishops, the Presbyterian Church in Canada, and The United Church of Canada (available from John Siebert, c/o Division of Mission in Canada, The United Church of Canada, 3250 Bloor Street West, Etobicoke ON M8X 2Y4).

VIDEO RESOURCES

Dancing the Dream (29:44 minutes). Produced by the Anglican Church of Canada, Anglican Video, for the Council for Native Ministries, 1993. Documents the national Native convocation at Minaki Lodge, Kenora, Ontario, August, 1993. Suitable for adults, small groups. A leader's guide is included.

The Healing Circle (55 minutes). Produced by Anglican Video. Includes traditional sacred healing rites of Native peoples as they struggle to overcome the legacy of residential school experience. Includes recorded proceedings of the Royal Commission on Aboriginal Peoples and interviews with Native leaders including Ovide Mercredi and traditional healer Sies'lom. Suitable for adults.

Search for Healing (24 minutes). Produced by the Anglican Church of Canada, Anglican Video for the Council for Native Ministries. Footage of Native children in residential schools. Includes stories of women who experienced both emotional and physical abuse. Suitable for use in church and school settings.

Notes

1 "Many and great, O God, are your works." In *Songs for a Gospel People*. (Winfield, British Columbia: Wood Lake Books, 1971), 80.

2 Deepak Chopra, *Journey Into Healing* (New York: Harmony Books, 1994), 18.

3 Excerpted from a reflection prepared for General Synod, 1992. At the reflection, Vi appeared in full ceremonial regalia, wearing the robe given to her by her family.

4 Excerpted from "Gitksan and Wet'suweten Society, A Primer," Vi Smith and Marie Wilson.

5 Excerpted from a reflection for leaders and Sunday School teachers, 1993.

6 Vi Smith is grateful to Leslie Barneswell, who shared these understandings of the Chinese language.

7 Excerpted from an Anglican Women's Conference in Calgary, Alberta, 1992.

RESOURCES

SARAH SIMON

Marsh, Winnifred. *People of the Willow: The Padlimuit Tribe of the Caribou Eskimo Portrayed in Watercolours.* Toronto: Oxford University Press, 1976. This is a beautiful and sensitive illustrated account by a missionary wife of her experience living with people of the Arctic. While her account is of the Keewatin area, west of Hudson Bay, there are many similarities in her experiences to those of missionary wives in the Mackenzie Delta.

McCarthy, Martha. *From the Great River to the End of the Earth: Oblate Missions to the Dene 1847–1921.* Edmonton: University of Alberta Press and Western Canadian Publishers, 1995. This book has detailed descriptions of the life of the Gwich'in around the time of the first contact with Europeans, their reliance on fishing to prepare for winter, their relations with the "Eskimo," and the role of the Hudson's Bay men and the missionaries in their changing lives.

Some background information for this story was provided by the Rt. Rev. John Sperry of Yellowknife, Northwest Territories (retired Bishop of the Arctic).

DR. JESSIE SAULTEAUX

Denig, Edwin Thomas. *Five Indian Tribes of the Upper Missouri: Sioux, Arikaras, Assiniboines, Crees, Crows.* Edited and with an introduction by John C. Ewers. Norman: University of Oklahoma Press, 1961. This book gives a historic account of some of the early habits of Assiniboine peoples as seen through the eyes of early member of the fur trade. While this book contains considerable cultural bias and a negative view of First Nations, its historic first hand descriptions of Assiniboine life and trials in the early 1800s are instructive and vivid.

Epes Brown, Joseph. Recorder and Editor *The Sacred Pipe: Black Elk's Account of the Seven Rites of the Oglala Sioux,* New York: Penguin Books, 1971. First published by University of Oklahoma Press, 1953.

Friesen, Gerald. *The Canadian Prairies: A History.* Toronto: University of Toronto Press, 1984. This book provides an excellent overview of the Assiniboine First Nation, its historic territories, development as intermediaries between fur traders and other Nations to the west and south, attempts to come to terms with oncoming settlement and development of Saskatchewan as a province of Canada.